MORE PRAISE FOR

Dakota: A Spiritual Geography

"[The Great Plains] is . . . a place where things timeless and deep can be found, offering gifts of grace and revelation, as Kathleen Norris so beautifully proves . . . 'Poets and Christians,' Norris writes, 'are people who believe in the power of words to effect change in the human heart.' In *Dakota* she clearly succeeds on both counts."

— Brad Knickerbocker, *Christian Science Monitor*

"By skillfully weaving together whatever material has come to hand . . . [Norris] has contrived a powerful evocation of an experience notoriously difficult to put into words."

— *The New Yorker*

"What a wonderful book . . . I enjoyed and admired it enormously. It's grandly funny, too, as part of its spiritual power . . . I loved the book."

— Annie Dillard

"Kathleen Norris's book on Dakota is especially nice, because it says something important, something that's close to my own feelings, and something that will give heart to a lot of people who find city life and industrial civilization hard to stomach."

— Wallace Stegner

"*Dakota* is an intelligent, thoughtful book written in a calming tone that encourages the contemplation of the importance of places: 'Not only to know where you are but to learn to love what you find there.'"

— *Cleveland Plain Dealer*

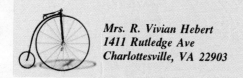
Kathleen Norris

DAKOTA

A Spiritual Geography

Houghton Mifflin Company

BOSTON • NEW YORK

For information about permission to reproduce
selections from this book, write to Permissions,
Houghton Mifflin Company, 215 Park Avenue South,
New York, New York 10003.

Library of Congress Cataloging-in-Publication Data

Norris, Kathleen, date.
Dakota : a spiritual geography / Kathleen Norris.
p.   cm.
Includes bibliographical references.
ISBN 0-395-63320-6
ISBN 0-395-71091-X (PBK.)
1. South Dakota — Civilization — 20th century. 2. North
Dakota — Civilization — 20th century. 3. Norris, Kathleen,
date. — Homes and haunts — Great Plains.   I. Title
F656.2.N66   1993   92-30820
978.3′ 03 — dc20   CIP

Printed in the United States of America

Book design by Robert Overholtzer

AGM 10 9 8 7 6

Excerpt from "Little Gidding" in *Four Quartets*, copyright 1943
by T. S. Eliot and renewed 1971 by Esme Valerie Eliot,
reprinted by permission of Harcourt Brace Jovanovich, Inc.,
and Faber and Faber Ltd.

In memory of Kathleen Dakota and Mary Beatrice

◆   ◆   ◆

"I think that if we examine our lives, we will find that most good has come to us from the few loyalties, and a few discoveries made many generations before we were born, which must always be made anew. These too may sometimes appear to come by chance, but in the infinite web of things and events chance must be something different from what we think it to be. To comprehend that is not given to us, and to think of it is to recognize a mystery, and to acknowledge the necessity of faith. As I look back on the part of the mystery which is my own life, my own fable, what I am most aware of is that we receive more than we can ever give; we receive it from the past, on which we draw with every breath . . . "

— Edwin Muir, *An Autobiography*

"Tell me the landscape in which you live, and I will tell you who you are."

— José Ortega y Gassett

CONTENTS

DAKOTA

THE BEAUTIFUL PLACES

The Scarecrow sighed. "Of course I cannot understand it,"
he said. "If your heads were stuffed with straw like
mine, you would probably all live in the beautiful places,
and then Kansas would have no people at all. It is
fortunate for Kansas that you have brains."
— L. FRANK BAUM, *The Wizard of Oz*

THE HIGH PLAINS, the beginning of the desert West, often
act as a crucible for those who inhabit them. Like Jacob's angel,
the region requires that you wrestle with it before it bestows a
blessing. This can mean driving through a snowstorm on icy
roads, wondering whether you'll have to pull over and spend
the night in your car, only to emerge under tag ends of clouds
into a clear sky blazing with stars. Suddenly you know what
you're seeing: the earth has turned to face the center of the
galaxy, and many more stars are visible than the ones we usually see on our wing of the spiral.

Or a vivid double rainbow marches to the east, following the
wild summer storm that nearly blew you off the road. The
storm sky is gunmetal gray, but to the west the sky is peach
streaked with crimson. The land and sky of the West often fill
what Thoreau termed our "need to witness our limits trans-
gressed." Nature, in Dakota, can indeed be an experience of
the holy.

More Americans than ever, well over 70 percent, now live in urban areas and tend to see Plains land as empty. What they really mean is devoid of human presence. Most visitors to Dakota travel on interstate highways that will take them as quickly as possible through the region, past our larger cities to such attractions as the Badlands and the Black Hills. Looking at the expanse of land in between, they may wonder why a person would choose to live in such a barren place, let alone love it. But mostly they are bored: they turn up the car stereo, count the miles to civilization, and look away.

Dakota is a painful reminder of human limits, just as cities and shopping malls are attempts to deny them. This book is an invitation to a land of little rain and few trees, dry summer winds and harsh winters, a land rich in grass and sky and surprises. On a crowded planet, this is a place inhabited by few, and by the circumstance of inheritance, I am one of them. Nearly twenty years ago I returned to the holy ground of my childhood summers; I moved from New York City to the house my mother had grown up in, in an isolated town on the border between North and South Dakota.

More than any other place I lived as a child or young adult — Virginia, Illinois, Hawaii, Vermont, New York — this is my spiritual geography, the place where I've wrestled my story out of the circumstances of landscape and inheritance. The word "geography" derives from the Greek words for earth and writing, and writing about Dakota has been my means of understanding that inheritance and reclaiming what is holy in it. Of course Dakota has always been such a matrix for its Native American inhabitants. But their tradition is not mine, and in returning to the Great Plains, where two generations of my family lived before me, I had to build on my own traditions, those of the Christian West.

When a friend referred to the western Dakotas as the Cappadocia of North America, I was handed an essential connection between the spirituality of the landscape I inhabit and that of the fourth-century monastics who set up shop in Cappadocia and the deserts of Egypt. Like those monks, I made a countercultural choice to live in what the rest of the world considers a barren waste. Like them, I had to stay in this place, like a scarecrow in a field, and hope for the brains to see its beauty. My idea of what makes a place beautiful had to change, and it has. The city no longer appeals to me for the cultural experiences and possessions I might acquire there, but because its population is less homogenous than Plains society. Its holiness is to be found in being open to humanity in all its diversity. And the western Plains now seem bountiful in their emptiness, offering solitude and room to grow.

I want to make it clear that my move did not take me "back to the land" in the conventional sense. I did not strike out on my own to make a go of it with "an acre and a cow," as a Hungarian friend naively imagined. As the homesteaders of the early twentieth century soon found out, it is not possible to survive on even 160 acres in western Dakota. My move was one that took me deep into the meaning of inheritance, as I had to try to fit myself into a complex network of long-established relationships.

My husband and I live in the small house in Lemmon, South Dakota, that my grandparents built in 1923. We moved there after they died because my mother, brother, and sisters, who live in Honolulu, did not want to hold an estate auction, the usual procedure when the beneficiaries of an inheritance on the Plains live far away. I offered to move there and manage the farm interests (land and a cattle herd) that my grandparents left us. David Dwyer, my husband, also a poet, is a New York City native who spent his childhood summers in the Adirondacks, and he had enough sense of adventure to agree to this. We expected to be in Dakota for just a few years.

It's hard to say why we stayed. A growing love of the prairie landscape and the quiet of a small town, inertia, and because as freelance writers, we found we had the survival skills suitable for a frontier. We put together a crazy quilt of jobs: I worked in the public library and as an artist-in-residence in schools in both Dakotas; I also did freelance writing and bookkeeping. David tended bar, wrote computer programs for a number of businesses in the region, and did freelance translation of French literature for several publishers. In 1979 we plunged into the cable television business with some friends, one of whom is an electronics expert. David learned how to climb poles and put up the hardware, and I kept the books. It was a good investment; after selling the company we found that we had bought ourselves a good three years to write. In addition, I still do bookkeeping for my family's farm business: the land is leased to people I've known all my life, people who have rented our land for two generations and also farm their own land and maintain their own cattle herds, an arrangement that is common in western Dakota.

In coming to terms with my inheritance, and pursuing my vocation as a writer, I have learned, as both farmers and writers have discovered before me, that it is not easy to remain on the Plains. Only one of North Dakota's best-known writers — Richard Critchfield, Louise Erdrich, Lois Hudson, and Larry

Woiwode — currently lives in the state. And writing the truth about the Dakota experience can be a thankless task. I recently discovered that Lois Hudson's magnificent novel of the Dakota Dust Bowl, *The Bones of Plenty*, a book arguably better than *The Grapes of Wrath*, was unknown to teachers and librarians in a town not thirty miles from where the novel is set. The shame of it is that Hudson's book could have helped these people better understand their current situation, the economic crisis forcing many families off the land. Excerpts from *The Grapes of Wrath* were in a textbook used in the school, but students could keep them at a safe distance, part of that remote entity called "American literature" that has little relation to their lives.

The Plains are full of what a friend here calls "good telling stories," and while our sense of being forgotten by the rest of the world makes it all the more important that we preserve them and pass them on, instead we often neglect them. Perversely, we do not even claim those stories which have attracted national attention. Both John Neihardt and Frederick Manfred have written about Hugh Glass, a hunter and trapper mauled by a grizzly bear in 1823 near the fork of the Grand River just south of Lemmon. Left for dead by his companions, he crawled and limped some two hundred miles southeast, to the trading post at Fort Kiowa on the Missouri River. Yet when Manfred wanted to give a reading in Lemmon a few years ago, the publicist was dismissed by a high school principal who said, "Who's he? Why would our students be interested?" Manfred's audience of eighty — large for Lemmon — consisted mainly of the people who remembered him from visits he'd made in the early 1950s while researching his novel *Lord Grizzly*.

Thus are the young disenfranchised while their elders drown

in details, "story" reduced to the social column of the weekly newspaper that reports on family reunions, card parties, even shopping excursions to a neighboring town. But real story is as hardy as grass, and it survives in Dakota in oral form. Good storytelling is one thing rural whites and Indians have in common. But Native Americans have learned through harsh necessity that people who survive encroachment by another culture need story to survive. And a storytelling tradition is something Plains people share with both ancient and contemporary monks: we learn our ways of being and reinforce our values by telling tales about each other.

One of my favorite monastic stories concerns two fourth-century monks who "spent fifty years mocking their temptations by saying 'After this winter, we will leave here.' When the summer came, they said, 'After this summer, we will go away from here.' They passed all their lives in this way." These ancient monks sound remarkably like the farmers I know in Dakota who live in what they laconically refer to as "next-year country."

We hold on to hopes for next year every year in western Dakota: hoping that droughts will end; hoping that our crops won't be hailed out in the few rainstorms that come; hoping that it won't be too windy on the day we harvest, blowing away five bushels an acre; hoping (usually against hope) that if we get a fair crop, we'll be able to get a fair price for it. Sometimes survival is the only blessing that the terrifying angel of the Plains bestows. Still, there are those born and raised here who can't imagine living anywhere else. There are also those who are drawn here — teachers willing to take the lowest salaries in the nation; clergy with theological degrees from

Princeton, Cambridge, and Zurich who want to serve small rural churches — who find that they cannot remain for long. Their professional mobility sets them apart and becomes a liability in an isolated Plains community where outsiders are treated with an uneasy mix of hospitality and rejection.

"Extremes," John R. Milton suggests in his history of South Dakota, is "perhaps the key word for Dakota . . . What happens to extremes is that they come together, and the result is a kind of tension." I make no attempt in this book to resolve the tensions and contradictions I find in the Dakotas between hospitality and insularity, change and inertia, stability and instability, possibility and limitation, between hope and despair, between open hearts and closed minds.

I suspect that these are the ordinary contradictions of human life, and that they are so visible in Dakota because we are so few people living in a stark landscape. We are at the point of transition between East and West in America, geographically and psychically isolated from either coast, and unlike either the Midwest or the desert West. South Dakota has been dubbed both the Sunshine State and the Blizzard State, and both designations have a basis in fact. Without a strong identity we become a mythic void; "the Great Desolation," as novelist Ole Rolvaag wrote early in this century, or "The American Outback," as Newsweek designated us a few years ago.

Geographical and cultural identity is confused even within the Dakotas. The eastern regions of both states have more in common with each other than with the area west of the Missouri, colloquially called the "West River." Although I commonly use the term "Dakota" to refer to both Dakotas, most of my experience is centered in this western region, and it seems to me that especially in western Dakota we live in tension between myth and truth. Are we cowboys or farmers? Are we fiercely independent frontier types or community builders? One myth that haunts us is that the small town is a stable place. The land around us was divided neatly in 160-acre rectangular sections, following the Homestead Act of 1863 (creating many section-line roads with 90-degree turns). But our human geography has never been as orderly. The western Dakota communities settled by whites are, and always have been, remarkably unstable. The Dakotas have always been a place to be *from:* some 80 percent of homesteaders left within the first twenty years of settlement, and our boom-and-bust agricultural and oil industry economy has kept people moving in and out (mostly out) ever since. Many small-town schools and pulpits operate with revolving doors, adding to the instability.

When I look at the losses we've sustained in western Dakota since 1980 (about one fifth of the population in Perkins County, where I live, and a full third in neighboring Corson County) and at the human cost in terms of anger, distrust, and grief, it is the prairie descendants of the ancient desert monastics, the monks and nuns of Benedictine communities in the Dakotas, who inspire me to hope. One of the vows a Benedictine makes is *stability:* commitment to a particular community, a particular place. If this vow is countercultural by contemporary American standards, it is countercultural in the way that life on the Plains often calls us to be. Benedictines represent continuity in the boom-and-bust cycles of the Plains; they incarnate, and can articulate, the reasons people want to stay.

Terrence Kardong, a monk at an abbey in Dakota founded

roughly a thousand years after their European motherhouse, has termed the Great Plains "a school for humility," humility being one goal of Benedictine life. He writes, "in this eccentric environment . . . certainly one is made aware that things are not entirely in control." In fact, he says, the Plains offer constant reminders that "we are quite powerless over circumstance." His abbey, like many Great Plains communities with an agricultural base, had a direct experience of powerlessness, going bankrupt in the 1920s. Then, and at several other times in the community's history, the monks were urged to move to a more urban environment.

Kardong writes, "We may be crazy, but we are not necessarily stupid . . . We built these buildings ourselves. We've cultivated these fields since the turn of the century. We watched from our dining room window the mirage of the Killdeer Mountains rise and fall on the horizon. We collected a library full of local history books and they belong here, not in Princeton. Fifty of our brothers lie down the hill in our cemetery. We have become as indigenous as the cottonwood trees . . . If you take us somewhere else, we lose our character, our history — maybe our soul."

A monk does not speak lightly of the soul, and Kardong finds in the Plains the stimulus to develop an inner geography. "A monk isn't supposed to need all kinds of flashy surroundings. We're supposed to have a beautiful inner landscape. Watching a storm pass from horizon to horizon fills your soul with reverence. It makes your soul expand to fill the sky."

Monks are accustomed to taking the long view, another countercultural stance in our fast-paced, anything-for-a-buck society which has corrupted even the culture of farming into "agribusiness." Kardong and many other writers of the desert West, including myself, are really speaking of values when they find beauty in this land no one wants. He writes: "We who are permanently camped here see things you don't see at 55 m.p.h. . . . We see white-faced calves basking in the spring grass like the lilies of the field. We see a chinook wind in January make rivulets run. We see dust-devils and lots of little things. We are grateful."

The so-called emptiness of the Plains is full of such miraculous "little things." The way native grasses spring back from a drought, greening before your eyes; the way a snowy owl sits on a fencepost, or a golden eagle hunts, wings outstretched over grassland that seems to go on forever. Pelicans rise noisily from a lake; an antelope stands stock-still, its tattooed neck like a message in unbreakable code; columbines, their long stems beaten down by hail, bloom in the mud, their whimsical and delicate flowers intact. One might see a herd of white-tailed deer jumping a fence; fox cubs wrestling at the door of their lair; cock pheasants stepping out of a medieval tapestry into windrowed hay; cattle bunched in the southeast corner of a pasture, anticipating a storm in the approaching thunderheads. And above all, one notices the quiet, the near-absence of human noise.

My spiritual geography is a study in contrasts. The three places with which I have the deepest affinity are Hawaii, where I spent my adolescent years; New York City, where I worked after college; and western South Dakota. Like many Americans of their generation, my parents left their small-town roots in the 1930s and moved often. Except for the family home in Honolulu — its yard rich with fruits and flowers (pomegranate, tangerine, lime, mango, plumeria, hibiscus, lehua, ginger, and bird-of-paradise) — and my maternal grandparents' house in a remote village in western Dakota — its modest and hard-won garden offering columbine, daisies and mint — all my childhood places are gone.

When my husband and I moved nearly twenty years ago from New York to that house in South Dakota, only one wise friend in Manhattan understood the inner logic of the journey. Others, appalled, looked up Lemmon, South Dakota (named for G.E. "Dad" Lemmon, a cattleman and wheeler-dealer of the early 1900s, and home of the Petrified Wood Park — the world's largest — a gloriously eccentric example of American folk art) in their atlases and shook their heads. How could I leave the artists' and writers' community in which I worked, the diverse and stimulating environment of a great city, for such barrenness? Had I lost my mind? But I was young, still in my twenties, an apprentice poet certain of the rightness of returning to the place where I suspected I would find my stories. As it turns out, the Plains have been essential not only for my growth as a writer, they have formed me spiritually. I would even say they have made me a human being.

St. Hilary, a fourth-century bishop (and patron saint against snake bites) once wrote, "Everything that seems empty is full of the angels of God." The magnificent sky above the Plains sometimes seems to sing this truth; angels seem possible in the wind-filled expanse. A few years ago a small boy named Andy who had recently moved to the Plains from Pennsylvania told me he knew an angel named Andy Le Beau. He spelled out the name for me and I asked him if the angel had visited him here. "Don't you know?" he said in the incredulous tone children adopt when adults seem stupefyingly ignorant. "Don't you know?" he said, his voice rising, "*This* is where angels drown."

Andy no more knew that he was on a prehistoric sea bed than he knew what *le beau* means in French, but some ancient wisdom in him had sensed great danger here; a terrifying but beautiful landscape in which we are at the mercy of the unexpected, and even angels proceed at their own risk.

Weather Report: January 17

◆

Encircled. The sea that stretched out before me in Maili, on the Waianae coast of Oahu, as this month began, has been transformed into the plains of North Dakota. I am riding a Greyhound bus to the small town where I'll be teaching writing to schoolchildren for the next two weeks. Snow in the fields has crusted over; wind-lines, restless as waves, flash like the ocean in sunlight.

"Never turn your back on the sea," is Hawaii's wisdom. "Or the sky," we Plains folk might add. Like sailors, we learn to read cloud banks coming from the west. We watch for sundogs and count rings around the moon.

I have turned with the circle: away from gentle air and birdsong, the Waianae Range unfolding like a fan in mist, toward a wind gritty with spent soil burning my tongue, a freezing rain that stings my hands and face.

In the schoolyard, a snow angel's wings are torn, caught in grass exposed by the sudden thaw. In the stuffy classroom, a little girl, restless and distracted, probably a bad student, becomes White Buffalo Calf Woman, speaking of a world in which all people are warm in winter and have enough to eat.

"They sing, 'the rain is new,' " she writes, " 'the rain is always new.' "

DESERTS

Dryness promotes the formation of flower
buds . . . flowering is, after all, not an aesthetic
contribution, but a survival mechanism.
— ANN HAYMOND ZWINGER, *The Mysterious Lands*

I'VE NEVER THOUGHT of myself as an ascetic. In fact, one of
my best friends has said that denying myself was never what
got me in trouble. But in acclimating myself to the bareness of
the Plains after the cornucopia of New York City I found to my
surprise that not only did I not lament the loss of urban stimulation, but I began to seek out even more deprivation than my
isolated prairie town of 1,600 could provide. I gave up watching
television, except for the Miss America Pageant and the Academy Awards (the former because there's always the chance that
the talent competition will include a baton twirler or a ventriloquist, or, better yet, a baton-twirling ventriloquist; the latter
because, though I've mostly given up movies as well, once a
year I like to see what people in Hollywood are wearing).

As living on the Plains has nudged me into a quieter life, I've
discovered that this is what I wanted. I've had to read more,
and more widely, so as not to become provincial, but interlibrary loans take care of me here. Reading is a solitary act, one
in keeping with the silence of the Plains, but it's also paradoxi-

cally public, as it deepens my connections with the larger world. All of this reflects a truth Thomas Merton once related about his life as a Trappist monk: "It is in deep solitude and silence that I find the gentleness with which I can truly love my brother and my sister."

The silence of the Plains, this great unpeopled landscape of earth and sky, is much like the silence one finds in a monastery, an unfathomable silence that has the power to re-form you. And the Plains have changed me. I was a New Yorker for nearly six years and still love to visit my friends in the city. But now I am conscious of carrying a Plains silence within me into cities, and of carrying my city experiences back to the Plains so that they may be absorbed again back into silence, the fruitful silence that produces poems and essays.

A side effect of this process has been a change in the way I feel when I'm in a crowd, a situation I now experience so rarely that I have the luxury of enjoying it. Several years ago, I traveled to New England to visit a friend who had terminal cancer. The journey took on the nature of a quest. First, the 125-mile trip over the prairie to the nearest airport, in Bismarck, North Dakota; a plane to Minneapolis and then LaGuardia, where I waited nearly two hours for my baggage; a bus into Manhattan; a taxi to Penn Station, where I stood for another two hours in a vast crowd — it was Labor Day weekend — waiting for a train.

It seemed as if all of the city's dense, humid heat was concentrated in that room, yet I felt at peace. The crowd was a typical urban mix: all races, young and old, rich and poor, sane and insane, quiet and ranting. As I stood in this group of strangers, I was happy to be one among many, and a powerful calm came over me. I began to see each of us as a treasure-bearer, carrying our souls like a great blessing through the world. After the relative emptiness of the Plains, partaking in such a feast of humanity was a blessing in itself.

In *Confessions of a Guilty Bystander* Thomas Merton writes of visiting Louisville on an errand for his monastery: "At the corner of Fourth and Walnut, in the center of the shopping district, I was suddenly overwhelmed with the realization that I loved all these people, that they were mine and I theirs, that we could not be alien to one another even though we were total strangers." I've come to see, as Merton says, that "it is the function of solitude to make one realize such things," and that it is the separateness of the Plains, like the separateness of the monastery, that teaches me that when I am in the city, "there are no strangers," and that "the gate of heaven is everywhere," even at Penn Station on Labor Day weekend.

Silence is the best response to mystery. "There is no way of telling people," Merton reminds us, "that they are all walking around shining like the sun." New Yorkers are told a great many things by strangers on the street, holy fools and mad alike. But the monk's madness is one that shows in the quiet life itself, with its absurd repetition of prayer and liturgy. It is "the madness of great love," in the words of one monk, that "sees God in all things," which nevertheless may be safely and quietly carried out of the monastery, into the world, and back again. As Basil Cardinal Hume, a Benedictine, has remarked, the monk is safe in the marketplace because he is at home in the desert.

Monks have long taken an ironic view of both themselves and the city. One ancient and playful story from the desert tradition tells of a disciple who was commanded by his Master for three years to give money to everyone who insulted him. When this period of trial was over the Master said to him: "Now you can go to Athens and learn wisdom." When the disciple was entering Athens he met a certain man who sat at the gate insulting everybody who came and went. He also insulted the disciple who immediately burst out laughing. "Why do you laugh when I insult you?" said the wise man. "Because," said the disciple, "for three years I have been paying for this kind of thing and now you give it to me for nothing." "Enter the city," said the wise man, "it is all yours."

I am not a monk, although I have a formal relationship with the Benedictines as an oblate, or associate, of a community of some sixty-five monks. As a married woman, thoroughly Protestant, who often has more doubt than anything resembling faith, this surprises me almost as much as finding that the Great Plains themselves have become my monastery, my place set apart, where I thrive and grow. It surprises me also to find that I no longer need to visit the city — any city — to obtain what I am missing, because I don't feel deprived. Sometimes I even seek out the desert within the city. On a recent trip to Manhattan, when a dinner date with an old friend fell through and I found myself with a free evening, I phoned some Episcopalian nuns I know and asked if I might come for vespers and dinner. While a Friday night rush hour swirled around us, we sang plainsong and then ate a meal in silence. It was what I needed to bring a hectic week to closure, a chance to recollect myself, to use a monastic term, and even to experience a bit of that peace that passes understanding.

It was the Plains that first drew me to the monastery, which I suppose is ironic, for who would go seeking a desert within a desert? Both Plains and monastery are places where distractions are at a minimum and you must rely on your own resources, only to find yourself utterly dependent on forces beyond your control; where time seems to stand still, as it does in the liturgy; where your life is defined by waiting.

No one waits better than monks, or farmers. The farmers and ranchers of western North Dakota can wait years for rain. I remember that at the height of a four-year drought, rain came only once all summer, on July 11 (a date I remember because it is the feast of Saint Benedict, and I got soaked walking to and from a hermitage). There was no precipitation again until a sparse snowfall came in November. By early August the grass had turned brown, as if it were late fall, and on windy days the dust was so bad you had to use headlights in the middle of the afternoon. Hope was about all we had.

Farmers and ranchers, whose hopes are so closely bound with the land, speak in terms of next-year country, a region that monks tend to see as encompassing all of eternity. For both farmer and monk, time is defined not by human agency but by the natural rhythms of day and night, and of the seasons.

The deprivations of Plains life and monastic life tend to turn small gifts into treasures, and gratitude is one of the first flowers to spring forth when hope is rewarded and the desert blooms. When the drought broke and gave us the wettest spring I've witnessed in eighteen years on the Plains, the exultant greenness of the land was enough to make people weep for joy. "Take a good look," one rancher said, "you may not see it like this again in your lifetime." The most pessimistic among us were reduced to muttering, "it won't last." We know it won't last, not in Dakota, and we stay anyway. That is our glory, both folly and strength.

For me, moving to Dakota meant entering a kind of literary desert. I left behind a job in arts administration in New York City that had allowed me to attend several poetry readings a week, and most of my friends were also writers. Disconnecting from all that has had consequences — I've been unable to get a grant for my writing since 1972, and I may be the only writer in America who's never been asked to work a summer writers' conference — but to be a monk means being still and at peace, at home in mind and body and at ease with one's place. When the deprivations of Dakota become oppressive, I try simply to accept what is the natural result of my choosing to live in isolated circumstances.

All in all, I suspect that the lack of a literary scene on the Plains has been good for me. I've developed as a writer in ways that might not have been possible in the literary hothouse of New York City. Now a poetry reading is an event in my life, a pleasure rather than something I take for granted. When I attend a good reading, experiencing what my former boss at the Academy of American Poets, Betty Kray, once called "the relief of hearing language," I find it as refreshing as a rain that drenches parched soil.

On the Plains I have also drunk in the language of un-schooled people, a language I was not much exposed to within the confines of the academic and literary worlds. Many farmers I know use language in a way that is as eloquent as it is grammatically unorthodox. Their speech often has great style; they never use the wrong word or make an error in phrasing. Magnificent old words like farrow, common English five hundred years ago, are still in use on the Plains. I even heard an old man use wain for wagon, a word that dates back to the Celts. Language here still clings to its local shading and is not yet totally corrupted by the bland usage of mass media. We also treasure our world-champion slow talkers, people who speak as if God has given them only so many words to use in a lifetime, and having said them they will die.

Plains speech, while nearly devoid of "-isms" and "-ologies," tends toward the concrete and the personal: weather, the land, other people. Good language for a poet to hear. And as my own language has become more grounded in Dakota, I've become a kind of evangelist for poetry, the exalted use of language. There is no ready-made audience for poetry in the western Dakotas, and I've delighted in discovering audiences in unlikely places: church suppers, grain elevator cooperative meetings, legislative committee sessions, political fundraisers, even a bull sale.

I find that prairie people are receptive to a broad range of contemporary poetry, although they'd be unlikely to cross town to attend a poetry reading at a college, were there a college in the vicinity. Their appreciation of the poems I've read aloud — from a broad spectrum of contemporary American poets — has given me a new understanding of the communal role of poets, a role poets have mostly abandoned by closeting themselves in academia. Surprises await poets who venture out into the larger community. For example, when my husband was elected to the Lemmon City Council, he found that his service included composing a new sewer ordinance, arguably the best written for many miles around.

My service to the public as a poet on the Plains has mainly

been in working as an artist-in-residence for the North Dakota Arts Council, a job that has taken me to schools in small towns throughout the state. My favorites are the one- to four-room country schools. One extremely windy spring day (in Dakota that means a steady 30 m.p.h., with gusts to 50 m.p.h.) a teacher drove me for miles along gravel section-line roads, off into nowhere, until we came to a one-room school in Slope County, North Dakota, planted between the aptly named Chalky Buttes and the Rainy Buttes, whose name must have been coined by a farmer in the throes of terminal optimism. It was one of our first warm days that year, and I could picture snakes coming out to sun themselves on those white rock ledges not far from the playground. In fact, the teacher kept a snakebite kit on her desk.

The students in such a school are often wary of visitors, particularly of one who wants to engage them in the suspicious act of writing. But when I've been able to read them literature about things they know, and talk about the reasons I write, what they come up with is gratifying: "I will own a ranch / of twenty horses, / all black stallions that look like silk, / and all of them mine." The best description I know of the Dakota sky came from a little girl at an elementary school on the Minot Air Force Base, a shy black girl who had recently moved from Louisiana and seemed overwhelmed by her new environment. She wrote: "The sky is full of blue / and full of the mind of God."

Once, near Williston, North Dakota, I worked in a rural district encompassing four country schools in over 1,100 square miles, an area around the size of Rhode Island. One of the schools, Round Prairie, was just that: surrounded by a view of grassland on all sides, it seemed like the quietest place on earth. In the early morning, before the school buses arrived, I would stand and watch the sunrise, listening for the few sounds that came; meadowlarks singing, wind stirring the grass, humming in a barbed-wire fence.

The constantly surprising encounters with children and the great treasure of their writing have seen me through many a dreary winter day. But the artist-in-residence program is also an experience of deprivation, another desert upon desert. I have to leave my home for weeks at a time, usually traveling two hundred miles or more to a town that might be too small to have a motel, so I'll board with a family, like a nineteenth-century schoolteacher. If there is a motel, it's often on its last legs, with a rusty tin shower stall and paper bath mat, and a pay phone in the parking lot. There's usually one café in town where I can get breakfast and dinner, though it closes at 6:30 P.M. Worse yet, in more "civilized" areas I might get a motel room with red and black flocked velvet wallpaper, making me feel as if I have stumbled into a New Orleans bordello in which I must somehow feel at home for the next two weeks.

The grim surroundings used to overwhelm me, and it was only when I began to apply what I had learned from the fourth-century desert monks I was reading that I found I could flourish there. I began to see those forlorn motel rooms as monks' cells, full of the gifts of silence and solitude. While this caused no end of amusement among the staff at the North Dakota Arts Council, it worked. Instead of escaping into television every night, I found that I could knit, work on my writing, and do serious reading; in short, be in the desert and let it bloom.

I had stumbled onto a basic truth of asceticism: that it is not necessarily a denigration of the body, though it has often been misapplied for that purpose. Rather, it is a way of surrendering to reduced circumstances in a manner that enhances the whole person. It is a radical way of knowing exactly who, what, and where you are, in defiance of those powerful forces in society — alcohol, drugs, television, shopping malls, motels — that aim to make us forget. A monk I know who directs retreats for other monasteries, and therefore must travel more than most Benedictines, has come to see air travel as a modern form of his ascetic practice. He finds the amenities offered, the instructions to relax and enjoy the flight laughable when he stops to realize where he is.

The insight of one fourth-century monk, Evagrius, that in the desert, most of one's troubles come from distracting "thoughts of one's former life" that don't allow us to live in the present, reflects what I regard as the basic principle of desert survival: not only to know where you are but to learn to love what you find there. I live in an American desert, without much company, without television, because I am trying to know where on earth I am. Dakota discipline, like monastic discipline, requires me to know. In a blizzard, or one of our sudden cold snaps that can take the temperature from thirty degrees above to thirty-five below in a matter of hours, not knowing can kill you.

Whether the desert is a monastery, a one-room schoolhouse forty miles from the nearest small town, where the children are telling you that "poetry's dumb," or a cinderblock motel room whose windows rattle in the fierce winter winds, a healthy ascetic discipline asks you to rejoice in these gifts of deprivation, to learn from them, and to care less for amenities than for that which refreshes from a deeper source. Desert wisdom allows you to be at home, wherever you are.

A brother came to Scetis to visit Abba Moses and asked him for a word. The old man said to him, "Go, sit in your cell, and your cell will teach you everything."

Weather Report: February 10

———◆———

I walk downtown, wearing a good many of the clothes I own, keeping my head down and breathing through several thicknesses of a wool scarf. A day so cold it hurts to breathe; dry enough to freeze spit. Kids crack it on the sidewalk.

Walking with care, snow barely covering the patches of ice, I begin to recall a canticle or a psalm — I can't remember which — and my body keeps time:

> Cold and chill, bless the Lord
> Dew and rain, bless the Lord
> Frost and chill, bless the Lord
> Ice and snow, bless the Lord
> Nights and days, bless the Lord
> Light and darkness, bless the Lord.

Another line comes to mind: "at the breath of God's mouth the waters flow." Spring seems far off, impossible, but it is coming. Already there is dusk instead of darkness at five in the afternoon; already hope is stirring at the edges of the day.

DAKOTA
Or, Gambling, Garbage, and the New Ghost Dance

THE DAKOTAS ARE America's Empty Quarter, with a population of about one and one third million people, roughly one fifth of the population of New York City, or a third that of Los Angeles, or a little less than half that of Chicago, spread over an area almost the size of California, and three times larger than New York State. Few appreciate the harsh beauty of a land that rolls like the ocean floor it once was, where dry winds scour out buttes, and the temperature can reach 110 degrees above or plunge to 30 below zero for a week or more. Say what you will about our climate, in Dakota we say it keeps the riff-raff out.

But Dakota bravado masks an anxiety that afflicts forgotten people in a mass-market society. We boast about our isolation, and the lengths we go to overcome it; I like to tell about the time I drove two hundred miles just to hear William Stafford read his poetry, and traveled two hundred miles home again that same night. We laugh when Bismarck, South Dakota, is mentioned on the national news. We shrug when North and South Dakota are routinely omitted from magazine advertisements for national stores and services.

We learn not to be surprised when the Environmental Protection Agency reports that big cities want to dump their garbage in our wide-open spaces. Given the dismal state of our economy, some Dakota towns are clamoring for the dollars the garbage industry would bring.

In several counties in North Dakota, a battle is raging between those who support an above-ground high-level nuclear waste facility to store spent nuclear fuel and those who do not trust federal safety standards and a county commissioner's claim that such a facility could be "clean, safe, and profitable." Also competing for this facility are Native American tribes in South Dakota and New Mexico. Like people in other depressed regions of the country, western Dakotans are so desperate for work that a job as a clerk or janitor in a nuclear dump sounds good. Here, it is the local farmers and ranchers who have taken the role of environmentalists in opposing the intrusion of nuclear waste into an area where they produce food. "We're part of the breadbasket of the world," one said, "and we'd hate to see that ruined."

It's not inspiring to have the Black Hills, the sacred *Paha Sapa* of the Lakota, classified as a "world-class site" by waste disposal companies, or to have the military move bomb-scoring sites onto our ranches. The Air Force still uses the steppes of western Dakota in what the locals used to call "practicing for Siberia"; low-flying bombers from the bases at Rapid City, Minot, and Grand Forks are a common sight on our prairie. My initiation came on a farm one day with a burst of noise and a huge plane flying over so low I could see the human form in the cockpit. "B-52," said the farmer, so used to it he didn't even look up. Now the planes are more often sleek B-1s.

For years the Plains have harbored many of the country's nuclear missile silos, several situated less than five miles from towns like Newell in South Dakota, or New Town in North

Dakota, population centers in their regions but expendable from a national perspective. Dakotans tend to support a strong military, and have paid for it by being placed at ground zero. It's a measure of the isolation people feel in western Dakota that now, as the missiles are being dismantled and their crews departing, some residents express regret. Ranchers generally found that the missile crews were good neighbors, and in an area where towns are more than forty miles apart, a good neighbor is hard to come by.

As happened during the Great Depression of the 1930s, which hit the Dakotas early in the 1920s with both a drought and collapsing grain prices, the economic crisis that the American people woke to at the end of 1991 struck the Great Plains in the 1980s. Times were so bad by 1985 that I began thinking of the Dakotas as the new Old South, an image that was reinforced when South Dakota dropped to fiftieth place among the states in average teacher salary, a position that Mississippi had held for years. We also began to surpass the South in harboring, on our Indian reservations, the poorest counties in the nation.

During the 1980s the Dakotas began to advertise for industry in much the way the Old South did, by offering low taxes along with reliable, semi-skilled workers who are used to living in a minimum-wage economy. A January 1992 ad in the Northwest Airlines magazine headed "Profit: see South Dakota" listed no corporate income tax, no personal income tax, no personal property tax, no business inventory tax, low workers' comp rates, low unemployment insurance rates, skilled labor, and high productivity as the attractions the state holds for business. Who does pay taxes in South Dakota? Anyone who owns real estate. A professional in South Dakota who earns $100,000 a year and rents a house or apartment is taxed directly only by a state sales tax of 4 percent, whereas a farm family on food stamps often pays a much higher percentage of its cash income in land taxes.

A 1983 article in *Forbes* on South Dakota's pursuit of out-of-state businesses was called "Let's Make a Deal," not inappropriate when you consider that it took the South Dakota legislature less than twenty-four hours to clear the way for Citibank to do business in the state, after the bank had fled New York's consumer-loan rate restrictions. Citibank quickly became South Dakota's fourth-largest employer. But many of South Dakota's new jobs are on the low end of the pay scale. In 1990, 36 percent of South Dakotans had an income below $15,000, nearly ten points over the national average. As a friend put it, "If we don't watch out, we'll become a Taiwan on the Prairie."

There are even uncanny echoes of the Old South in the literary world, where it's always been more acceptable to be from the South than from South Dakota. In the 1980s, books set on the Plains, some by writers living there, began to receive regular mention in the *New York Times Book Review*. But the price of this acceptance may prove high. It's the mythologized Old South that's acceptable to readers outside that region, and this may prove true for Dakota as well. We could be facing a situation like that of Native Americans who came to be seen as romantic while their culture was being destroyed. Indian children were punished for speaking their own language, but Indian words and symbols were appropriated to sell a myth of freedom on the American road. Pontiac, Cherokee, even the sacred Thunderbird.

I watched uneasily as a "Dakota chic" surfaced in America in the mid-80s, in both tony urban restaurants and national advertising campaigns. Dakota Beer came on the market in 1986 with ads focused on "wheat from the heartland and the people who grow it." The ads were filmed in Montana, but as one South Dakota official put it, with typical self-effacement, "at least they came to within a state of us." That same year, Lee Iacocca, wearing a white cowboy hat, introduced the Dodge Dakota pickup truck, and the corporation flew real Dakota cowboys and Indians to Hollywood to pose for ads. It's ironic that in the year the beer came out, the *Rapid City Journal* reported that over 20 percent of South Dakota's farmers, the good folk growing that wheat, either left or seriously contemplated leaving their land for economic reasons, and so many auto and farm imple-ment dealers closed their doors that people would have had to drive a hundred miles or more to buy the truck, if they could afford it. That year, in the 576xx Zip Code area, the median household income was $15,670. (Currently it stands at $17,660.)

A sense of loss has begun to haunt those residents of western Dakota whose immigrant ancestors prospered after coming to the Plains in the late nineteenth and early twentieth centuries. Less visible than the poor in urban areas, they are afflicted by physical isolation in particularly severe ways. People who are laid off in my town have to travel one hundred miles to a Job Service office in order to register for benefits, and there is no public transportation on the route.

Ironically, Lemmon was less isolated fifty years ago, when passenger trains stopped here. In the 1930s my mother could take the train from Lemmon to college in Chicago, and for a time in the late 1950s United Airlines had scheduled flights in and out of Lemmon. In 1950 the town had a population of nearly 2,800; down to 1,600 today, we're still the largest town by far in northwestern South Dakota, an area nearly twice the size of Massachusetts.

Our nearest public transportation is a Greyhound flag stop at a gas station ninety miles north, but if I'm going south, east, or west, the distance is two hundred miles or more. Many communities now offer, with government assistance, limited public transportation that mainly serves senior citizens who need to visit regional medical centers. But deregulation during the 1980s made travel here much more expensive and difficult.

With small towns shrinking and services eroding, many Dakotans retain an appalling innocence about what it means to be rural in contemporary America. The year we lost our J. C. Penney store, young people were quoted in the town's weekly newspaper as saying they'd like to see a McDonald's or a K Mart open in its place. Somehow they have not grasped that in modern American capitalism, which they defend vociferously in the annual American Legion Auxiliary essay contest, the market is everything. Since there is no market here, nothing that counts demographically, we don't exist.

I've long had the feeling that our inability to influence either big business or big government is turning all Dakotans into a kind of underclass. Native Americans are by far the poorest and most invisible among us; but in the lopsided distribution of population (in both states, 35 to 40 percent of the people live in the counties along the eastern border, including 20 percent who live in the counties where Fargo and Sioux Falls are located), western Dakotans are increasingly invisible to more affluent eastern Dakotans, and Dakotans as a whole are invisible to the rest of America.

In self-defense, many rural Dakotans have become more

insular and self-absorbed, more isolated in spirit, and the thin veneer of Dakota pride is more painfully evident. A recent study of North Dakota entitled *Vision 2000* found people suffering from both low self-esteem and increasing suspicion of others. Small-town people are often suspicious of the professionals who move to the Plains; "if they were any good, they'd be working in a bigger place" is how the reasoning goes.

The mixed messages of Dakota pride can be spectacular. The popular wisdom declares that this is God's country and New York City is a hellhole, yet a rumor plagued me when I moved here: it was said that the only way I could collect a sizeable (and largely fictional) inheritance from my grandparents was to leave New York and come to Lemmon.

Current economic realities make such mixed messages a burden, especially for our young. In Lemmon, it's become unusual for high school graduates to venture outside the region to go to college. Yet parents must raise their children for the world outside; there are few job opportunities here. And the young are both rewarded and punished for defecting: proud parents make sure that the local paper prints stories about their children's activities in college, but on returning home for the summer, these students often find they've become outsiders on their home ground.

Like ethnic peoples all over the world, Dakotans are in danger of becoming victims of their own mythology. As our towns are failing and our lives here become less viable, many Dakotans cling stubbornly to a myth of independence and local control that makes it difficult for us to come together and work for the things that might benefit us all. We've been slow to recognize that our traditional divisiveness (country versus town, small town versus city) makes us weak, not strong. As one North Dakota official recently put it, "We talk about a global society . . . for crying out loud, we have to open our eyes and become a state society first."

In fact, the ruggedly independent Dakotas have always been more or less a colony in America, remarkably dependent on outside interests. I feel it every time I sell wheat for less than it costs to produce, or when I sell the grass-fed cattle of my grandparents' herd to be fattened and pumped full of chemicals in a feed-lot. Our cherished idol, local control, makes us more, not less, vulnerable to manipulation by outside interests. When the farm crisis deepened in the mid-1980s and First Bank Systems pulled out of Lemmon, the article in our weekly newspaper spoke about how wonderful it was that local people were going to have the chance to invest in and run their own bank. In the Minneapolis *Tribune* the bank's move out of small towns such as ours was described as enabling it to provide more "sophisticated consumer services" to urban and suburban Minnesotans. The *Wall Street Journal* applauded First Bank's decision as part of a strategy to drop agricultural loans.

The Dakotas make a curious colony for America, but the mystique has been there at least since 1876, when Custer rode out of Mandan to his doom, and Wild Bill Hickok was shot in a saloon in Deadwood. Later on, the young Teddy Roosevelt tried out the life of a cowboy in the North Dakota Badlands. Fueled by dime novels and western movies, most recently *Dances With Wolves* and *Thunderheart*, the appeal of Dakota has never died out, and is apparently inexhaustible in Europe, judging from the number of starstruck Europeans who venture across Highway 12 every summer, passing through Lemmon on their way to Montana or the Black Hills.

For those of us who have a healthy respect for summer heat

waves and the violent storms they generate, the Dakota mystique can wear thin in a hurry. One year I visited a carpenter friend who was building houses and a Mormon church on the Standing Rock Indian Reservation. The two Mormon missionaries were from Hawaii; suffering in the dry heat, they clearly had no idea what the Dakota climate would have in store. For some reason the area was also blanketed that summer by Jehovah's Witnesses, and some Dutch tourists had moved into a haystack near my friend's trailer. They stayed on even after a nearby haystack was hit by lightning.

I prize the hiddenness of Dakota, and have grown protective of the silence here — the places that have become sacred to me, that in all likelihood few humans have ever walked. When I was in Honolulu over Christmas, visiting my family shortly after *Dances With Wolves* came out, I went to parties where I was astonished to hear people discussing South Dakota. "I had no idea it was so lovely," one elegant woman said. "I never thought about South Dakota at all. Now I'd like to see it." *No*, I had to keep myself from saying, *you can't*. Unconscionably, because the state is poor and needs an economic boost, I find myself wanting to keep the professional tourists out.

But tourism is the base of many colonial economies, and the Dakotas have begun to pursue visitors aggressively, offering gambling as a lure. Nearly every storefront along the main street in Deadwood now houses a casino, and the Lower Brule Sioux tribe recently built a giant gambling emporium in eastern South Dakota. More tribes are jumping on the bandwagon; the Mdewakanton Sioux operate a casino in neighboring Minnesota with spotlights that come together in the shape of Dakota teepee poles visible in the sky for thirty miles. But this, along with the region's fledgling waste industry, is not particularly good for our self-esteem. Nor is it likely to alter the traditional boom-and-bust economy of the region. And there's always the danger that in selling Dakota to tourists, we'll destroy it. I've lived in Hawaii, after all, and have seen what tourism can do to the soul of a place.

Dakotans know why they like living here, where life is still lived on a human scale. I've banked in New York City and know what a luxury it is to be able to write a counter-check (a blank check on which I write in my own account number) at stores within one hundred miles of home (roughly the distance between New York City and Philadelphia or Los Angeles and Santa Barbara). And small-town Dakotans currently have the luxury of a falling crime rate. Of course our population is falling as well, but it can be pleasant to live in a place such as Lemmon, where arrests dropped by a third between 1981 and 1991. Most arrests were made for traffic violations, though we had five burglary arrests in 1985, down to one in 1990 and none in 1991. There have been two murders in the county since I moved there in 1974, and both were family affairs, the killing of old men for their money. It may be odd to think of living in Dakota as a luxury, but I'm well aware that ours is a privileged and endangered way of life, one that, ironically, only the poor may be able to afford.

Among the simple pleasures of Dakota is driving where there's no traffic. One moonlit night late in the fall, my husband and I left Rapid City and traveled the two hundred miles home seeing fewer than fifteen vehicles and well over a hundred antelope. Most days I take a long walk at sunrise, and sometimes I'm greeted with a spectacular moonset as well, the western horizon on fire. There's no sound to speak of except for wind and birdsong. I can hear a car coming from miles away.

I've walked through miniature Grand Canyons few humans have ever seen, through sweeps of land that put John Ford vistas, and even the scenery in *Dances With Wolves*, to shame. Our odd, tortured landscape terrifies many people. Some think it's as barren as the moon, but others are possessed by it. "The land lives," is how one young rancher put it to me. But now that the Minneapolis/St. Paul metropolitan area contains more people than Montana and the Dakotas combined, I fear that his attitude will prove incomprehensible to modern, urban Americans who live as if they have outgrown the land that feeds them, as incomprehensible as a similar reverence for the land among Native Americans was to the railroad barons, merchants, and immigrant farmers of a century ago.

In western Dakota, as in few other places I've seen in this country, one realizes the truth of Gertrude Stein's remark "In the United States there is more space where nobody is than where anybody is." Eleven counties in South Dakota now meet the traditional definition of frontier, places having two or fewer persons per square mile. This is two more than in 1980, and 52 of the state's 67 counties are still losing residents at a rapid rate.

We're addicted to growth in America, and those figures look like failure. Similar demographics in other Plains states have led Frank and Deborah Popper, professors at Rutgers University, to wonder if it wouldn't be better to move young ranchers off the land they love and get them to do something more useful in the smog of a big city. They have proposed turning much of the Plains into a buffalo commons, a government reserve inhabited by wildlife, buffalo herds, perhaps a few

nomadic Indian tribes (and, given the reality of American politics, probably a dumping ground for radioactive and other toxic
waste). Rural counties in states from North Dakota to Texas
with too small, too old, or too poor a population would go into
the commons.

After little more than a century of white settlement, are the
Great Plains still a frontier? Are they in fact inhabitable? The
Poppers' thesis suggests that this has not been answered to this
nation's satisfaction, and that makes one's life here all the more
precarious. In 1974, when I was asked to write an essay about
my move from New York City to Lemmon, I wrote of being
haunted by the sense that we are all Indians here, as much in
danger of losing our land as the Indians of one hundred years
ago. And if it happens, I fear we will meet with the same
massive national indifference.

I do not wish to minimize the particular sufferings that have
been and continue to be inflicted on Native Americans, but the
farm crisis of the 1980s leads me to believe I was on to something. And others have made the same connection. I once
heard a Lakota holy man say to college students at the University of North Dakota, "Farmers are the next Indians, going
through the same thing we did." The students had been rude
to him, carrying on conversations while he spoke. He was just
an old man, just an Indian who described himself as an unem-
ployed plumber. But when he asked, "How many of us are
going to stand beside the farmer and see justice done for these
people?" there was silence in the room. At least a few of the
students, the ones from farms, had wondered that themselves.

In the Ghost Dance religion of just a hundred years ago, a
desperate people tried to assimilate Christianity into their native religion. They believed that their ancestors would come

back to help them in their fight against white soldiers and settlers; their warriors wore shirts they believed the soldiers' bullets could not penetrate. Though this seems tragic to Western eyes, some Lakota credit the Ghost Dance with helping them preserve their ancient religious traditions over the last century. Others have found in it a viable blend of Christianity and the old religion. "I'm a good Catholic," one elderly woman told me, "and I also carry the pipe."

The situations are not parallel and comparisons are risky, but I wonder if a new kind of Ghost Dance isn't arising on the prairie among whites who take refuge in conspiracy theories and fundamentalist churches that shut their doors to the outside world. They gather in a circle and sing holy songs to bring back the past, when prairie towns were flooded with settlers, songs that will keep at bay outsiders' laws and weapons and talk of hazardous waste dumps. Their hope, wrested from literal interpretations of the Bible, lies not in living in this world but escaping into another.

The Plains are not forgiving. Anything that is shallow — the easy optimism of a homesteader; the false hope that denies geography, climate, history; the tree whose roots don't reach ground water — will dry up and blow away.

PATAGONIA

People of Perkins County . . . live on the sediment
of what was the edges of a giant inland sea that
covered the interior of the nation.
— DAVID J. HOLDEN, *Dakota Visions*

ONCE, IN A LIBRARY in South Dakota, I found an old book
of poems about Patagonia, and felt right at home.

We too are dry and "wind-bullied," remote, our grassland
suitable for sheep and cattle and little else. We know the bitter trade-offs that the poet Katharine Ellis Barrett describes in
"Sacrifice:"

> There's grass enough.
> The winter drifts lay late.
> Under one
> Five hundred starved.
> They'd eaten tails and wool.
> If there had been less snow
> Five thousand must have starved this summer.

We, too, need moisture so badly we're glad to see it even
when it comes in violent storms, the tranquility of a summer
afternoon shattered by rolling thunder from the west carrying
with it sheets of rain and hailstones large enough to cut off
heads of grain or even kill young calves caught in open range.

As the ice pellets melt in the wreckage of field or garden, we manage to be grateful for even this bitter pill.

The effect of dryness on living tissue is in evidence all around us: hollow skulls of mice and gophers, cetaceous fossils along a river bank, a leaf imprint in sandstone. Petrified wood and grass speak to us of the deep past, of forest and swamp and inland sea. Fossils of oysters, sea turtles, and the chambered nautilus are often found near the tops of buttes. Bones of Triceratops, Brontosaurus, and Tyrannosaurus rex dot the prairie, and in southern Perkins county, fossilized dinosaur tracks wander off in search of a retreating ocean.

What makes the western plains seem most like the ocean to me is not great sweeps of land cut into swells and hollows, or the grass rippling like waves (what the Lakota call greasy grass), or the sheets of rain that one sees moving in the distance like storms at sea. It is the sound.

Many mornings, when the wind has come up during the night, the trees around my house thunder like high surf that swells and ebbs without cease.

In open country, far from any trees, the wind beats against you, as insistent as an ocean current. You tire from walking against it just as you would from swimming against an undertow. Working outdoors on such a day leaves you dizzy, and your ears will still be ringing at night, long after you have drawn the shelter of four walls around you.

The wind can be a welcome companion on a hot day, but even die-hard Dakotans grow tired when the sky howls and roars at forty miles an hour for a day or more. The wind is so loud you have to shout at the person next to you, and you can't hear yourself think at all. You begin to wonder if you have a self.

There is no escape: the western Dakotas are the windiest region in the lower forty-eight states. An old woman I know who has lived all her life on ranches here and rarely complains about deprivations (she raised a family with no electricity or running water, and can remember winnowing wheat by hand with blankets in the 1920s because her family could not afford to hire a threshing machine and crew) once said to me, "The one thing I could never stand was the wind."

Wind yanks moisture out of the ground, turning wet fields to dust in a matter of hours; it robs farmers of valuable crops at harvest, blowing them away with the dust of the combine. It encircles us, much as water encircles an island, increasing our sense of isolation. The wind is what drove many homesteaders off the land. It drove some of them mad.

For me, walking in a hard Dakota wind can be like staring at the ocean: humbled before its immensity, I also have a sense of being at home on this planet, my blood so like the sea in chemical composition, my every cell partaking of air. I live about as far from the sea as is possible in North America, yet I walk in a turbulent ocean. Maybe that child was right when he told me that the world is upside-down here, and this is where angels drown.

Listening to the voice of the sky, I wonder: how do we tell our tales, how can we hope to record them? I'd like to believe that deep in our bones the country people of Dakota, like poets, like monks, are, as Jean Cocteau once said of poetry, "useless but indispensable."

A STARFISH IN MOTT

An abba said, 'The prophets wrote books, then came our
fathers who put them into practice. Those who came
after them learnt them by heart. Then came the
present generation, who have written them out and put
them into their window seats without using them.'
— *The World of the Desert Fathers*

THE GIRL has scarcely looked at me. She's been drawing and
writing furiously all during class. When the bell rings she
hurries up to me with more than twenty sheets of paper. She's
Indian — Hidatsa, maybe, or Sioux — and the other children
let her pass as if she were invisible.

The morning star dances in a red circle, singing a song about
his girlfriend Sheila; the angel Gabriel stands before Mary, his
blue wings ablaze with stars. His mouth is open wide and
notes are coming out, each one a different color. A woman with
green hair holds her hands up to the sky and says:

> These are secret words,
> Say them after me.
> May all the plants and flowers rise
> And all people rise from death.

I look up from the paper: a dusty shelf, a starfish in a jar
caked with dust beside dusty petri dishes. I see shades of
blue: the globe cerulean, the sky bleached out. And out the

window, above the children's heads, topsoil, the residue of ancient oceans, swirling like a thumbprint in the playground, wind pushing the empty swings.

"So many poems," I say, smiling at the girl. "You must love to write." She shifts from foot to foot and weaves her hands in air. "I don't have paper at home," she says, "so I keep them in my head. That's where they live until I write them down."

Weather Report: March 25

◆

Mud and new grass push up through melting snow. Lilacs in bud by my front door, bent low by last week's ice storm, begin to rise again in today's cold rain. Thin clouds scatter in a loud wind.

Suddenly, fir trees seem like tired old women stooped under winter coats. I want to be light, to cast off impediments, and push like a tulip through a muddy smear of snow. I want to take the rain to heart, let it move like possibility, the idea of change.

GATSBY ON THE PLAINS

"You can't repeat the past."
"Can't repeat the past?" he cried incredulously. "Why
of course you can!"
— F. Scott Fitzgerald, *The Great Gatsby*

IN THE SPRING of 1984 a woman in her early thirties said to me: "You don't understand this town because you're an outsider. You don't know what it was like here twenty years ago. That's what we want; that's what we have to get back to."

Beyond the shock of hearing a young woman say she wanted to recapture the earthly paradise the world had seemed at twelve, I began thinking: 1964. The nation was still reeling from the assassination of John F. Kennedy. Our involvement in Vietnam was greater than most Americans yet recognized, and escalated that year with the Tonkin Gulf Resolution and sending U.S. bombers over Laos. Congress passed the Civil Rights Act after a long and bitter struggle, but Southern blacks had to fight to be seated at the Democratic convention, and civil rights workers Schwerner, Goodman, and Cheney were murdered by white vigilantes in Mississippi. College girls like me, if we knew women's history at all, thought that the women's suffrage movement had ended because, once women won the vote, all its goals were obtained.

But paradise existed in a little Dakota town, where it seemed that the dreams of progress held by the homesteaders and early merchants were at last being realized. Commodity prices were good, and a federal dam project boosted the economy. New churches and a school were being built, but the boom was not so great that stability was threatened. You could still get baptized, married, and eulogized surrounded by your own.

As the woman went on talking, I felt both grief and anger. Grief, after all, is the pain of loss, and this woman was taking away both the hard lessons and the progress of twenty years; the road from Selma to Jesse Jackson's speech at the 1984 Democratic Convention. From women in terrible isolation, beginning to doubt not their own sanity but the sanity of the "feminine" role demanded of them, to a dynamic feminism with many victories, in both law and social attitudes; if nothing else, it got women wearing more sensible shoes. Even 1968, with its assassinations and tragic Democratic convention; or the Vietnam war, or Watergate — had all this meant nothing? Would we really be better off pretending none of it had happened? Or that it had all taken place in another world, having no effect on our own?

I began to wonder where her magic boundaries lay: family? town? the state line? Even I, who have roots here, who spent my childhood summers learning to swim in the WPA pool, playing Monopoly with neighborhood children on a picnic table in my grandparents' backyard, am to her an outsider, a serpent in her Eden, because in defining the town's problems, I refer to the world outside it: the national economy, regional demographics. I'd spent too long exposed to the world outside to really love the town she longs to see as a Norman Rockwell portrait come to life, a triptych with neat white edges. Dad is at work, Mom is at home, and the rosy-cheeked kids are spending their allowance at the soda fountain on Main.

What she's forgetting is that the soda fountain is gone, along with the drug store it was a part of. It's one of several empty buildings on Main. Paradise wasn't self-sufficient after all, and the attitude and the belief that it ever was is part of the reason it's gone.

Change has not often been kind to the Dakotas. While Dakota boosters in the late nineteenth century predicted confidently that the population of each state would rise to a million by 1900, neither state has ever come close. The current North Dakota population is 660,000; for South Dakota, 715,000. Perkins County, which includes Lemmon, is typical of counties west of the Missouri River in that during the twentieth century its population base has been slowly ebbing away; 11,348 at the height of the homestead boom in 1910; 7,055 in 1925; 5,530 in 1945; 4,700 in 1980; and 3,932 in 1990.

Illusions of progress that allowed North Dakota to enter the 1915 Panama–Pacific Exposition in San Francisco with an exhibit entitled "North Dakota Enlightens the World" soon gave way, in the 1920s and the "Dirty Thirties," to farm and small business bankruptcies and the hard economic realities of the Dust Bowl. Change is still resented on the Plains, so much so that many small-town people cling to the dangerous notion that while the world outside may change drastically, their town does not. Population may shrink, as it has in Lemmon, from 3,400 in 1964 to around 1,600 today, with a median age older than most of America. But when myth dictates that the town has not really changed, ways of adapting to new social and economic conditions are rejected: not vigorously, but with a strangely resolute inertia. In today's troubled agricultural economy this translates into a death wish, and values that once served to protect and preserve the town become threats to its survival.

In the early 1980s this inertia made it hard for many rural Dakotans to recognize and respond to changing economic realities. Our town has lost many businesses in the last twenty years, but the idea that an industrial development committee should be formed seemed preposterous to many. Their attitude was: Why seek out industry? We've never had to do it before. Why band together to give new businesses a break? We were never given any breaks. They called the others doomsayers.

They were indulging in a willful ignorance of their own regional history. Ghost towns surround us, but the boom years beginning in the 1950s had allowed a false sense of security to take hold. We told ourselves that the process that ruined these little towns was over, that our town had a pristine existence outside of history, exempt from the dynamics of economic and social change. Given this attitude, it was impossible for us to gauge the severity of the farm crisis that struck in the 1980s.

When businesspeople did form an industrial development committee, there was talk of bringing light industry in. But aspirations were scaled down almost immediately. As in the past, several businesses were kept out by dog-in-the-manger businessmen and investors who didn't want enterprises established by outsiders. "We have to keep the wage scale down," one told a county commissioner. While this is an understandable concern for any small business, in the western Dakotas such attitudes have hindered economic development so greatly as to be self-defeating. The young wage earners move away.

One small manufacturing plant was created by local investors, but the committee's efforts went mainly toward attracting small-scale businesses that aren't likely to survive unless major employers are also brought in. We got a craft shop, a gunsmith, an upholsterer, a dry cleaner, and a shoe repair shop to replace the ones we had lost. The new cleaner folded in less than six months, but the Chamber picked the theme "Alive, Well, and Growing" for its annual banquet without any sense of irony, and many were comforted by the boosterism. There had been too much talk lately about how the town was going downhill. The economic development group collapsed not long after that, and it was several years before another one rose from its ashes.

That is not too dramatic a metaphor. Combatting inertia in a town such as Lemmon can seem like raising the dead. It is painful to watch intelligent businesspeople who are dedicated to the welfare of the town spend most of their energy combatting those more set in their ways. Community spirit can still work wonders here — people raised over $500,000 in the hard times of the late 1980s to keep the Lemmon nursing home open, and a much-needed sewer bond issue passed by a 98 percent margin — but in the long run inertia has a way of destroying not only our self-confidence but our sense of community.

Small towns pride themselves on their sense of community, the neighborliness which lack of anonymity is supposed to provide. When everyone knows everyone else, the theory goes, community is highly valued. This is evident when disaster strikes. A farmer hospitalized in early summer finds that his neighbors have put up his hay. A new widow's kitchen fills with friends and acquaintances who bring food, coffee, memories, and healing.

But the fault line of suspicion and divisiveness exposed by the farm crisis in the mid-1980s has left wounds that have not healed, making me wonder how real community is in my town and perhaps in other isolated Dakota towns that have seen three or four generations pass.

It is a given that isolated Plains communities cannot hold on to most of the best and brightest who grow up there. After college they move on to better job opportunities elsewhere. Of course, many who come back to run a family business or ranch are as bright and enterprising as those who opt to leave, but even these people have a difficult time maintaining a normal sense of the world "outside." They may start out regarding their isolation as a hardship that is worth enduring for the benefits of raising a family in a small town or in the country. But the isolation begins to exact an unforeseen toll, making them more provincial than they'd intended to be. They stop connecting to the world outside, except through the distorting lens of television. They drop subscriptions to national magazines and newspapers. Their curiosity about the world diminishes.

By the time a town is seventy-five or one hundred years old, it may be filled with those who have come to idealize their isolation. Often these are people who never left at all, or fled back to the safety of the town after a try at college a few hundred miles from home, or returned after college regarding the values of the broader, more pluralistic world they had encountered as something to protect themselves and their families from.

As their frame of reference diminishes, so do their aspirations and their ability to adapt to change. To some extent,
wariness about change is a kind of prairie wisdom. The word's
origins lie in the marketplace, as in "exchange," and negative
connotations abound, like "to shortchange" or deceive. But the
sad truth is that the harder we resist change, and the more we
resent anyone who demands change of us, the more we shortchange ourselves. Who could be more impoverished than the
man who, on hearing news of a former teacher, exclaimed in a
tavern, "That old cow? She used to make me read. Said I
couldn't graduate till I read all she wanted. Well, I showed her;
I haven't read a book since."

Many teachers here also seem to give up any thought of
lifelong learning. More than once I've wondered, looking at
signatures on old book cards when I worked at the library, why
so many adults in a town like Lemmon stop reading. More than
once I've been surprised to discover that people who show no
sign that they've ever read a book in their lives, are in fact
former teachers, college graduates from the days when an education was said to mean something.

Even the young here can come to view the world as static.
High school students asked in the early 1980s to prepare a
résumé for a mock job application replied: "Why? We'll never
live anyplace big enough to have to do this." When such attitudes come to prevail in a town, family is still important but
community may not be. Because it can't look outward, the
town begins to turn in on itself, and a schismatic, ultimately
self-defeating dynamic takes hold. This is what struck many
western Dakota towns when the farm crisis of the mid-1980s
took hold.

Most economists regard this crisis as the worst for farmers since the 1920s and 1930s. In the fall of 1984 the *Wall Street Journal* ran an excellent series on the farm economy that covered agricultural lenders, implement dealers, and farmers who were going under, as well as those who had changed their operations to meet changing times and were doing well. Reading about one such successful farmer made me realize how ill equipped most farmers I knew were for adjusting to the international world of modern agriculture.

Here is an Ohio farmer:

> A globe on his desk is a reminder that he must think of world-wide supply and demand, of distant politics and climates. These global factors figure strongly in his marketing now that America faces greatly heightened competition for world grain trade. Successful farmers today must have international savvy. The Richards family does. Dinner table talk is as apt to dwell on Brazil's weather as Ohio's. [They] subscribe to the *Financial Times* of London. Their bathroom reading is a magazine called *International Economic Indicators*.

There are farmers and ranchers here who are well informed on the world events that affect them. But many are like a family I knew: when I helped paint some outbuildings on their place and wanted to get newspaper to use as a drop cloth, I had to settle for pages from a Sears catalog. "A newspaper!" exclaimed a friend from town. "Where do you think you are!" That family went bankrupt; the husband is now working as a welder. And the insular thinking that helped to put them under continues to reign: only a handful of people have read the copies of Dan Morgan's *Merchants of Grain* or Gilbert Fite's *American Farmers: The Last Minority* that have been in the library

for years. Some troubled farm families who could benefit from
Fite's analysis of the process by which America's agricultural
majority of 96 percent in 1790 became a minority of 30 percent
by 1920 and a mere 1.7 percent today choose instead to believe
in conspiracies by Jewish bankers.

More than ever, I've come to see conspiracy theories as the
refuge of those who have lost their natural curiosity and ability
to cope with change. Is it any wonder that the world seems full
of strange and implacable forces to someone who doesn't know
how to look up a Zip Code, use a computerized card catalog,
or even make a long-distance phone call? When my husband
tended bar in Lemmon, he was often asked to place calls for
people flustered by a pay phone. The night he telephoned a
research library at a university in California to settle a barroom
dispute about the planets is now part of local legend. He might
as well have been a shaman.

The ranchers here who do keep current on issues that affect
them have adopted a "wait and see" attitude toward the towns
around them. They know not all of them will make it. One is
more likely to find realistic economic and social attitudes
among farmers and ranchers and in the tiniest Dakota towns
(those with populations of under a thousand) than in larger
ones.

The smallest towns have made do with so little for so long
they count themselves lucky to have a post office, a gas station,
a general store, and perhaps a tavern; they have no illusions
that they are necessary to the farm economy. But such illusions
have flourished in towns like Lemmon that are just large
enough to have a merchant class and a real society to which
farm people may or may not belong, depending on who and

how successful their parents were and whether or not they wear their manure-caked boots into town. In the mid-1980s I watched small-town society react to the farm crisis with a volatile mixture of fear and denial, and an unfortunate tendency to blame the victim. Of course, one of the things people were busy denying is the extent to which they had become victims as well.

Several articles in the *Journal* series concerned the devastating effects the farm crisis was having on the economic and social structure of small towns. A prediction was made that no town with a population under 1,000 would survive as a viable economic trade center. But the news roused little interest here. As late as 1985, copies of such articles presented at local industrial development committee meetings were left on tables, unclaimed and unread. The attitude was that whatever was being said was being said by outsiders and therefore applied to other places, not to us.

When it became obvious that local farmers were indeed in trouble, and a county sheriff retired early rather than serve foreclosure papers on a relative, fears began to surface in town among businessmen worried for their livelihood and retired people worried about an eroding tax base. But no sense of community helped them face these fears honestly or directly. Instead, it seemed that the habit of insular thinking had become so deeply ingrained that many townspeople couldn't help but turn the farmers in trouble into a new class of outsiders from which the town had to be protected. The fact that these outsiders were now neighbors a few miles down the road and no longer strangers in Detroit or Los Angeles only made people resent them more. Some even began talking as if the town didn't need those dumb old farmers anyway, as if its survival weren't tied to an agricultural base. "They got themselves in this mess, let them get themselves out," was one remark I heard.

The saddest story I know was of an encounter between two "insiders," one a longtime town resident, the wife of a retired rancher, the other the patriarch of one of the oldest farm families in the area. The man had been working desperately during what was supposed to be his retirement in an attempt to keep his son from going bankrupt. "There is no farm crisis," the woman told him firmly in her spotless living room only fifteen miles from his farm but a world apart.

The *Wall Street Journal* articles had been easy to dismiss because they came from the outside world. A favorite local saying is "an expert is someone who's fifty miles from home," and while this has a certain folksy charm, it also reveals a smug refusal to use expert witness even when it might be in your best interest to do so. When even local families can be turned into outsiders and enemies, ministers and other professionals make easy targets. They set themselves up for attack simply by doing their jobs, organizing stress and suicide prevention workshops and support groups for bankrupt farmers. When this happened in Lemmon, some townspeople complained that the ministers were only making things worse with their negative talk.

Many teachers, doctors, lawyers, and ministers in rural towns are outsiders. And they often find that they've moved to a place in which professional standards have slipped over the years. Some of this is a welcome relaxation of urban standards, as simple as the bank president not wearing a tie to work. We bend the rules; that's part of small-town charm. The danger is that professional standards will slip so far that people not only accept the mediocre but praise it, and refuse to see any outside standards as valid.

Year after year, state auditors find the same errors in the way city books are kept, recommending that "accounting records as set forth in the Municipal Accounting Manual be established." If eventually a change is made, most likely it will be forced on us and resented, blamed on government interference. A teacher enters a student in a speech contest without checking the correct pronunciation of the many French words in his talk, and is annoyed when told that this must be done if the student is to enter a regional competition. A well-educated newcomer is hired as a church treasurer and fired a year later for trying to push her ideas on the finance committee, which couldn't conceive of building an endowment but wanted to invest only in passbook savings and certificates of deposit, as it always had. One complaint made about her was that she came to meetings too well organized.

Such outsiders can unwittingly pose a threat to the existing social order, and if their newcomers' enthusiasm doesn't wear off, if their standards don't fall to meet the town's, and especially if they keep on trying to share what they know, they have to be discouraged, put down, or even cast out.

Small-town people know that professionals, especially those who have or seek exceptional credentials, are likely to live among them for a short time before moving on to a place where they can earn more money and advance their careers. Their differentness often shows in needs that cannot be met locally. A clergyman, for instance, who is in the process of obtaining a Ph.D. from Claremont in ancient biblical studies is able to live in Lemmon only because the South Dakota State Library can provide through interlibrary loan the hundreds of books and articles he needs, including texts in Ethiopic, free of charge.

With such services becoming commonplace, others might consider living in a remote area and commuting electronically to their workplaces. But the changes wrought by new information technology are not always welcome here. In one town, when the state library offered a public library access through a computer hook-up to millions of books in regional and national databases, the librarian did not want it. It seemed like an insult to her many years of dedicated service, suggesting that the decent but small collection of books she'd built was no longer good enough. Interlibrary loan is an unwelcome link to a larger world, forcing us to recognize that we're not as self-sufficient as we imagine ourselves to be.

Small-town insecurity often takes the form of an exaggerated sense of our own importance. A minister here was criticized, in an anonymous letter to her superiors at the state level, for doing volunteer work for the American Cancer Society. As a survivor of a particularly deadly form of cancer, she had been honored by the Society and asked to take on some speaking engagements in the area. She saw this as a valid form of ministry. But her critics couldn't imagine that her work might reflect well on their church; all they could see was that she was taking time away from them. By these standards, if being honored by the Cancer Society is bad, receiving the Nobel Peace Prize would be much worse.

When outsiders genuinely like the area despite a difference in background and lifestyle so great that townspeople can't pretend they are really "just like us," a new and disruptive dynamic enters the picture and resentments flourish. Newcomers may find that their interest and enthusiasm is mistrusted. I remember one minister who came here with a Ph.D. in biblical studies from Princeton Theological Seminary. He was over-qualified for rural ministry, but grew to love the Plains. A few years into his ministry he found that one of his parishioners, a teacher, had nursed a grudge against him ever since his first visit to her family. She felt he had talked down to her.

"He asked us about our cattle," she complained. "Didn't he realize that I'm well educated, too?" Her master's degree in speech communications from a state teachers' college had established her as an intellectual, something she took very seriously, referring to nonprofessionals, and even teachers without master's degrees, as "laypeople." That degree was supposed to guarantee her status forever, even if all she read any more was the latest James Michener novel.

The minister was supposed to ask her about Michener, not cattle, and they would have an intellectual conversation. It never occurred to her that an intelligent outsider might assume that cattle are important in the West River of Dakota, even to a teacher whose husband is a rancher. Sadly, the woman might have learned from the minister about the Bible, as he had tried to learn from her about cattle.

Instead, she joined ranks with other threatened insiders who were determined to expel this outside force from the community. Attacking him at a church council meeting a few days after the minister was released from the hospital following surgery, a young man who had served on the pastor search committee said bitterly, "the only reason we took you was because we were desperate." This remark was both comic and pathetic, and the minister must have felt as if he'd stepped, like Alice, through the looking glass. This church could barely afford the minimum salary required by its denomination, and as an experienced pastor he could easily have earned twice the salary elsewhere. In fact, he had turned down the pastorate of a 2,000-member Chicago church in order to take the small-town call. He was learning the truth of the old saying "no good deed goes unpunished." In Dakota he was told: you preach our way, or not at all.

His situation reflected an advanced stage of the process by which a small town's values come to supersede and ultimately reverse those of the world outside. A community in which this has occurred is a very fragile one, and needs to see itself as idyllic in contrast to the bad world outside. This kind of insider / outsider thinking has been well documented in history. There is both irony and schism built into a system that uses expulsion as a means of preserving its unity.

A small town in this situation sometimes seems to have fallen under an evil spell. A Catholic priest who serves several North Dakota communities is quoted in Richard Critchfield's recent *Trees, Why Do You Wait?* as saying, "Ever since I've been [here] it seems like every year somebody gets crucified. It's usually centered on the school . . . Every year someone seems to stir up controversy, calumny. It's vicious. It's depressing." He adds, "Someone in that community has got to stand up and say, 'Do you think we could be nice to each other this week?' "

Outsiders who leave such a town do so under a cloud: it's been true of teachers, doctors, and clergy in Lemmon for many years. Often they are turned into scapegoats by a group that can't face its own internal differences. As Mary Douglas writes in *Natural Symbols:* "In a community in which overt conflict cannot be contained, witchcraft fears are used to justify expulsion and fission. These are communities in which authority has very weak resources."

Sometimes the weakness of authority in a small town is a good thing; it makes life easier. But constant turnover (in Lemmon in a recent seven-year period, four churches went through eight ministers, and the school ran through six principals and four superintendents) weakens our institutions, not the professionals who are forced out. They tend to get better jobs elsewhere.

It is the community that suffers when it refuses to validate any outside standards, and won't allow even the legitimate exercise of authority by the professionals it has hired. This is a serious problem in the western Dakotas. Pastors are expected to attend women's Bible study meetings, but sometimes are resented when they make comments designed to stimulate discussion, as the women are used to simply reading aloud the printed lessons. A teacher was told by a school administrator to stop teaching Shakespeare because "the kids don't need it." She got her revenge by teaching *Antigone* instead. Another experienced teacher, who loved working in a small town not far from Rapid City, was criticized for her big-city wardrobe and for inspiring an interest in poetry and drama among her rural charges. Her contract wasn't renewed. A woman found she couldn't get twenty people to sign up for a program sponsored by the South Dakota Humanities Council, in which for a nominal fee people would receive several paperbacks and admission to lectures by visiting scholars. She had thought it might work: the series was on the Dakota heritage, and among the books were Rolvaag's *Giants in the Earth* and *Black Elk Speaks*. She was told by the leader of one group she approached: "We decided we already had enough books."

Small towns need a degree of insularity in order to preserve themselves. But insularity becomes destructive when ministers, teachers, and librarians grow weary of pretending not to know what they know, and either leave or cease to offer themselves as resources whose knowledge could benefit the community. It's depressing to see how the years of tumultuous turnover and unresolved conflicts dictate how a newcomer will fare before he or she has even arrived in town. The last time we were looking for a new school superintendent I heard a long-time resident say, "I hope they don't get someone who wants to change everything."

G. Keith Gunderson, who was raised in the rugged sheep country of Harding County, South Dakota, and has served as a Lutheran minister here for most of his life, grasps the ethos of western Dakota better than anyone I know. He understands the deep resistance to change that is embedded in the prairie consciousness and once wrote in a letter to me:

> We need outsiders here but often end up repelling them, especially professionals, especially ministers. I have heard glowing praise turn into bitter fire within a few short years. Prairie people know they do this. And hidden in their rejection . . . is a seed by which they set themselves up to be exploited and then abandoned, over and over again.

People in this condition become unable to distinguish between outsiders who would exploit them and those who could help. But as times get harder in the West River of Dakota, I suspect that a town's ability to utilize the talents, resources, and insights of outsiders will be key to its survival.

Monasteries know this: they make provision for frequent visitations by abbots or prioresses of other houses who conduct confidential interviews with every member of the community and have a wide range of authority. They can mandate immediate changes, such as sending an abbot or other community official to an alcohol treatment program, requiring that business records be kept in a more precise manner, or demanding that a formation director (the monk in charge of training the community's newest members) be replaced. They can comment on any aspect of community life, from the quality of food to the quality of liturgy.

Small towns in Dakota that claim to be communities would do well to emulate monasteries in this regard. But the ability to receive outside criticism predicates a self-critical ability that I wonder if small towns in Dakota have ever had. It's hard for us to grasp the paradox the North Dakota priest sees in *Trees, Why Do You Wait?*, that "it's outside influence that really seems to stabilize a community." Instead, we resist all outside influence in order to make our institutions what we want them to be, and end up creating institutions that are mediocre and unstable.

Eventually it becomes difficult to find even old-timers willing to lead the Chamber of Commerce or run for city office. They burn out fast in the face of hard work and constant criticism and are made to feel foolish for having tried to improve things. To risk change is to risk being attacked on your home turf or, more ominously for small-town businesspeople, having controversy threaten your livelihood. And what of community? In the small Dakota town, the luxury of knowing those with whom we do business has largely atrophied our ability to deal with any issue larger than personality. When property taxes rise, we don't look to a failing economy and the town's dwindling population for the reason, we write anonymous letters to the newspaper complaining about those who work for the city or the school. And when these officials ask us to respond to economic reality by consolidating services, or even, God forbid, entering into a cooperative venture with another small town, we take it personally. At a loss, we look for someone to blame for these drastic changes.

Ironically, it is the town's cherished ideal of changelessness that has helped bring about the devastation, and it is the town's true history that is lost. An incoming president of a church committee may find that no one has bothered to keep minutes for years. A new school librarian may decide to take to the dump the only bound copies of the high school newspaper, dating from the 1920s. She'll not know that the volumes would have been gladly received by either the public library or the local historical society because she has only a vague knowledge of them. The school administrators and faculty, in orienting her to the town, most likely did not mention them. We don't like to connect here. ·

We don't need to connect. The prairie landscape isolates us from each other as well as from our history. Gunderson finds a darkness here that says: "Progress is illusion and hope is folly. We are born, we live, we die. Leave us alone." He writes: "We who live in western Dakota look forward to the day when we will rest in some forlorn prairie cemetery with relatives and friends around us, the land and the weather forcing us to live in light of that reality: we belong to the land." The land does not change, or does so only slowly; maybe Dakotans emulate the land in that respect. The danger is that in so doing they can lose an important aspect of their humanity. In forsaking the ability to change, they diminish their capacity for hope.

We don't need change. What we need, as my friend suggested, is to turn back the clock to the way things were twenty years ago, when the town was booming and the world made sense. There was nothing that couldn't be judged by the values we all shared. But she may find, as Gatsby did, that disconnecting from change does not recapture the past. It loses the future.

Weather Report: April 14

◆

Just before dawn all is blue: I barely see the lark bunting light on a fence post. I stop to admire its white, plump breast, and for a moment the two of us are alone in this world, and at peace.

The bunting flies away: white on black on white on black. Fields to the west are touched with gold, pale gold with a cast of red.

Suddenly I have a shadow, a clown on stilts who stretches across the road, down along the ditch and into the field, dark as a crow. Around my shadow is a nimbus of light; I walk in grass tipped with gold.

Above the monastery a huge cloud hovers, wings outstretched from a scrawny neck, as ungainly as the flying dinosaurs I pored over in adolescence, relieved to find creatures even homelier than I. The cloud pulls apart, and with it the great pterosaur. Its descendants the meadowlarks sing briskly all around me.

Today's reading, for the second Sunday of Easter, is from the Book of Acts: "those who believed shared all things in common." This dream, like the apostles and dinosaurs who once roamed the earth performing signs and wonders, is not quite extinct. There is hope, as Miss Dickinson called it, "the thing with feathers." There is my soul like a bird.

CLOSED IN

GULLS AND FOG ARE among the things in the West River of Dakota that remind us that this was once an inland sea. The gulls follow farmers as they would follow fishing boats, diving for mice and gophers unearthed by the plow or dislodged by the swather that cuts grain and hay.

The fogs, as dense as any I've seen on the New England coast, descend during the night and sometimes don't lift for a day or more. We're not used to being closed in, to having our big sky fall on us, and it makes us nervous.

Sometimes the sky falls for real, four or five days of dry snow that tries to fall and is lifted by the wind to fall again and again. In a bad blizzard you can lose sight of the house across the street, and four-wheel drives get stuck in town. Nothing moves in the country, though I did have a young cowboy friend who took off on his horse at the start of one of our spring blizzards and rode to where his herd was calving. He moved into an old barn and for three days rode out after the newborns, carrying them back across his saddle while the mothers, bellowing, followed him through the drifts to shelter. He spent Easter cooking and washing out long johns in water from melted snow, and celebrated saving his calves with a few swigs from a whiskey bottle.

Being closed in makes us edgy because it reminds us of our vulnerability before the elements; we can't escape the fact that life is precarious. A friend in her early forties once gave birth to a premature baby during an ice storm. Everyone knew it was going to be a rough delivery, even before the anesthesiologist got fogged in at an airport eighty miles away. He drove on glare ice, but it took over four hours to get to the hospital, and by that time a healthy baby had been delivered by cesarean section without anesthesia.

The sky can close in on you fast in Dakota, rain turning to snow, then to heavy snow and wind in a matter of a few minutes — or miles, if you're unlucky enough to be caught on the road. In a true whiteout, you drive with one hand on the steering wheel and the other on the car door, which you open a crack to try to see the median line through the blowing snow. If there is another person in the car, they do the same, using the white shoulder line, mile markers, and fence posts as guides to keep the car on the road.

It's surprising how far a person can drive this way. My husband and I managed about fifty miles once in just over three hours, going east of Aberdeen on Highway 12. We had planned to travel more than four hundred miles that day, driving east and then south to Sioux Falls for a South Dakota Arts Council meeting. When a whiteout descended on us after Aberdeen, we still had 150 miles to go. Coming to Interstate 29, a north–south route, we had a choice: If the wind was blowing the snow off the surface of the road, we could take it, if not, it was another seven miles or so to a place where we could spend the night.

Getting out near Summit, so named because at 2,000 feet it is the highest point between the Mississippi and the Missouri rivers, I faced the wind, ate snow, laughed, and suddenly relaxed. It was glorious to be in a world in which the sky and land had merged, where everything was painted in shades of white. No sense of distance, of depth or height; just a few fence lines, trees, and telephone poles to give perspective. It was a world of great beauty and stillness.

A semi truck roared by on I-29, heading south. The road was slushy but we could see it, so we went on.

THE HOLY USE OF GOSSIP

It is the responsibility of writers to listen to gossip and pass
it on. It is the way all storytellers learn about life.
— GRACE PALEY

If there's anything worth calling theology, it is listening to
people's stories, listening to them and cherishing them.
— MARY PELLAUER

I ONCE SCANDALIZED a group of North Dakota teenagers
who had been determined to scandalize me. Working as an
artist-in-residence in their school for three weeks, I happened
to hit prom weekend. Never much for proms in high school, I
helped decorate, cutting swans out of posterboard and sprinkling them with purple glitter as the school gym was festooned
with lavender and silver crepe paper streamers.

On Monday morning a group of the school outlaws was
gossiping in the library, just loud enough for me to hear, about
the drunken exploits that had taken place at a prairie party in
the wee hours after the dance: kids meeting in some remote
spot, drinking beer and listening to car stereos turned up loud,
then, near dawn, going to one girl's house for breakfast. I
finally spoke up and said, "See, it's like I told you: the party's
not over until you've told the stories. That's where all writing
starts." They looked up at me, pretending that it bothered
them that I'd heard.

"And," I couldn't resist adding, "everyone knows you don't get piss-drunk and then eat scrambled eggs. If you didn't know it before, you know it now." "You're not going to write about *that*, are you?" one girl said, her eyes wide. "I don't know," I replied, "I might. It's all grist for the mill."

When my husband and I first moved to Dakota, people were quick to tell us about an eccentric young man who came from back East and gradually lost his grip on reality. He shared a house with his sheep until relatives came and took him away. "He was a college graduate," someone would always add, looking warily at us as if to say, we know what can happen to Easterners who are too well educated. This was one of the first tales to go into my West River treasure-house of stories. It was soon joined by the story of the man who shot himself to see what it felt like. He hit his lower leg and later said that while he didn't feel anything for a few seconds, after that it hurt like hell.

There was Rattlesnake Bill, a cowboy who used to carry rattlers in a paper sack in his pickup truck. If you didn't believe him, he'd put his hand in without looking and take one out to show you. One night Bill limped into a downtown bar on crutches. A horse he was breaking had dragged him for about a mile, and he was probably lucky to be alive. He'd been knocked out, he didn't know for how long, and when he regained consciousness he had crawled to his house and changed clothes to come to town. Now Bill thought he'd drink a little whiskey for the pain. "Have you been to a doctor?" friends asked. "Nah, whiskey'll do."

Later that night at the steak house I managed to get Bill to eat something — most of my steak, as it turned out, but he needed it more than I. The steak was rare, and that didn't sit well with Bill. A real man eats his steak well done. But when I said, "What's the matter, are you too chicken to eat rare meat?" he gobbled it down. He slept in his pickup that night, and someone managed to get him to a doctor the next day. He had a broken pelvis.

There was another cowboy who had been mauled by a bobcat in a remote horse barn by the Grand River. The animal had leapt from a hayloft as he tied up a horse, and he had managed to grab a rifle and shoot her. He felt terrible afterwards, saying, "I should have realized the only reason she'd have attacked like that was because she was protecting young." He found her two young cubs, still blind, in the loft. In a desperate attempt to save them he called several veterinarians in the hope that they might know of a lactating cat who had aborted. Such a cat was found, but the cubs lived just a few more days.

There was the woman who nursed her husband through a long illness. A dutiful farm daughter and ranch wife, she had never experienced life on her own. When she was widowed, all the town spoke softly about "poor Ida." But when "poor Ida" kicked up her heels and, entering a delayed adolescence in her fifties, dyed her hair, dressed provocatively, and went dancing more than once a week at the steak house, the sympathetic cooing of the gossips turned to outrage. The woman at the center of the storm hadn't changed; she was still an innocent, bewildered by the calumny now directed at her. She lived it down and got herself a steady boyfriend, but she still dyes her hair and dresses flashy. I'm grateful for the color she adds to the town.

Sometimes it seems as if the whole world is fueled by gossip. Much of what passes for hard news today is the Hollywood fluff that was relegated to pulp movie magazines when I was a girl. From the Central Intelligence Agency to *Entertainment Tonight*, gossip is big business. But in small towns, gossip is still small-time. And as bad as it can be — venal, petty, mean — in the small town it also stays closer to the roots of the word. If you look up gossip in the *Oxford English Dictionary* you find that it is derived from the words for God and sibling, and originally meant "akin to God." It was used to describe one who has contracted spiritual kinship by acting as a sponsor at baptism; one who helps "give a name to." Eric Partridge's *Origins*, a dictionary of etymology, tells you simply to "see God," and there you find that the word's antecedents include gospel, godspell, *sippe* (or consanguinity) and *"sabha*, a village community — notoriously inter-related."

We are interrelated in a small town, whether or not we're related by blood. We know without thinking about it who owns what car; inhabitants of a town as small as a monastery learn to recognize each other's footsteps in the hall. Story is a safety valve for people who live as intimately as that; and I would argue that gossip done well can be a holy thing. It can strengthen communal bonds.

Gossip provides comic relief for people under tension. Candidates at one monastery are told of a novice in the past who had such a hot temper that the others loved to bait him. Once when they were studying he closed a window and the other monks opened it; once, twice. When he got up to close the window for the third time, he yelled at them, "Why are you making me sin with this window?"

Gossip can help us give a name to ourselves. The most revealing section of the weekly *Lemmon Leader* is the personal column in the classified ads, where people express thanks to those who helped with the bloodmobile, a 4-H booth at the county fair, a Future Homemakers of America fashion show, a benefit for a family beset by huge medical bills. If you've been in the hospital or have suffered a death in the family, you take out an ad thanking the doctor, ambulance crew, and wellwishers who visited, sent cards, offered prayers, or brought gifts of food.

Often these ads are quite moving, written from the heart. The parents of a small boy recently thanked those who had remembered their son with

> prayers, cards, balloons, and gifts, and gave moral support to the rest of the family when Ty underwent surgery. . . . It's great to be home again in this caring community, and our biggest task now is to get Ty to eat more often and larger amounts. Where else but Lemmon would we find people who would stop by and have a bedtime snack and milk with Ty or provide good snacks just to help increase his caloric intake, or a school system with staff that take the time to make sure he eats his extra snacks. May God Bless all of you for caring about our "special little" boy — who is going to gain weight!

No doubt it is the vast land surrounding us, brooding on the edge of our consciousness, that makes it necessary for us to call such attention to human activity. Publicly asserting, as do many of these ads, that we live in a caring community helps us keep our hopes up in a hard climate or hard times, and gives us a sense of identity.

Privacy takes on another meaning in such an environment, where you are asked to share your life, humbling yourself before the common wisdom, such as it is. Like everyone else, you become public property and come to accept things that city people would consider rude. A young woman using the pay phone in a West River café is scrutinized by several older women who finally ask her, "Who are you, anyway?" On discovering that she is from a ranch some sixty miles south, they question her until, learning her mother's maiden name, they are satisfied. They know her grandparents by reputation; good ranchers, good people.

The *Leader* has correspondents in rural areas within some fifty miles of Lemmon — Bison, Chance, Duck Creek, Howe, Morristown, Rosebud (on the Grand River), Shadehill, Spring Butte, Thunder Hawk, White Butte — as well as at the local nursing home and in the town of Lemmon itself, who report on "doings." If you volunteer at the nursing home's weekly popcorn party and sing-along, your name appears. If you host a card party at your home, this is printed, along with the names of your guests. If you have guests from out of town, their names appear. Many notices would baffle an outsider, as they require an intimate knowledge of family relationships to decipher. One recent column from White Butte, headed "Neighbors Take Advantage of Mild Winter Weather to Visit Each Other," read in part: "Helen Johanssen spent several afternoons with Gaylene Francke; Mavis Merdahl was a Wednesday overnight guest at the Alvera Ellis home."

Allowing yourself to be a subject of gossip is one of the sacrifices you make, living in a small town. And the pain caused by the loose talk of ignorant people is undeniable. One couple I know, having lost their only child to a virulent pneumonia (a robust thirty-five year old, he was dead in a matter of days) had to endure rumors that he had died of suicide, AIDS, and even anthrax. But it's also true that the gossips don't know all that they think they know, and often misread things in a comical way. My husband was once told that he was having an affair with a woman he hadn't met, and I still treasure the day

I was encountered by three people who said, "Have you sold your house yet?" "When's the baby due?" and, "I'm sorry to hear your mother died."

I could trace the sources of the first two rumors: we'd helped a friend move into a rented house, and I'd bought baby clothes downtown when I learned that I would soon become an aunt. The third rumor was easy enough to check; I called my mother on the phone. The flip side, the saving grace, is that despite the most diligent attentions of the die-hard gossips, it is possible to have secrets.

Of course the most important things can't be hidden: birth, sickness, death, divorce. But gossip is essentially democratic. It may be the plumber and his wife who had a screaming argument in a bar, or it could be the bank president's wife who moved out and rented a room in the motel; everyone is fair game. And although there are always those who take delight in the misfortunes of others, and relish a juicy story at the expense of truth and others' feelings, this may be the exception rather than the rule. Surprisingly often, gossip is the way small-town people express solidarity.

I recall a marriage that was on the rocks. The couple had split up, and gossip ran wild. Much sympathy was expressed for the children, and one friend of the couple said to me, "The worst thing she could do is to take him back too soon. This will take time." Those were healing words, a kind of prayer. And when the family did reunite, the town breathed a collective sigh of relief.

My own parents' marriage was of great interest in Lemmon back in the 1930s. My mother, the town doctor's only child, eloped with another Northwestern University student; a musician, of all things. A poor preacher's kid. "This will bear watching," one matriarch said. My parents fooled her. As time went on, the watching grew dull. Now going on fifty-five years, their marriage has outlasted all the gossip.

Like the desert tales that monks have used for centuries as a basis for a theology and way of life, the tales of small-town gossip are often morally instructive, illustrating the ways ordinary people survive the worst that happens to them; or, conversely, the ways in which self-pity, anger, and despair can overwhelm and destroy them. Gossip is theology translated into experience. In it we hear great stories of conversion, like the drunk who turns his or her life around, as well as stories of failure. We can see that pride really does go before a fall, and that hope is essential. We watch closely those who retire, or who lose a spouse, lest they lose interest in living. When we gossip we are also praying, not only for them but for ourselves.

At its deepest level, small-town gossip is about how we face matters of life and death. We see the gossip of earlier times, the story immortalized in ballads such as "Barbara Allen," lived out before our eyes as a young man obsessively in love with a vain young woman nearly self-destructs. We also see how people heal themselves. One of the bravest people I know is a young mother who sewed and embroidered exquisite baptismal clothes for her church with the memorial money she received when her first baby died. When she gave birth to a healthy girl a few years later, the whole town rejoiced.

My favorite gossip takes note of the worst and the best that is in us. Two women I know were diagnosed with terminal cancer. One said, "If I ever get out of this hospital, I'm going to look out for Number One." And that's exactly what she did. Against overwhelming odds, she survived, and it made her mean. The other woman spoke about the blessings of a life that had taken some hard blows: her mother had killed herself when she was a girl, her husband had died young. I happened to visit her just after she'd been told that she had less than a year to live. She was dry-eyed, and had been reading the Psalms. She was entirely realistic about her illness and said to me, "The one thing that scares me is the pain. I hope I die before I turn into an old bitch." I told her family that story after the funeral, and they loved it; they could hear in it their mother's voice, the way she really was.

Weather Report: May 19

◆

You make the winds your messengers. — *Psalm 104*

Sunday morning, 5 A.M. First light touches the tops of trees, and in the muddy parking lot of the bar west of town a bride leans into the window of a car, talking to a couple inside. She holds her veil in her hands. A late-model pickup, louder than it has to be, roars into the lot. Three young men get out, one still in his rented tux — and cowboy hat, of course. They drop their beer cans into a pile. A wedding in the West.

I keep moving and don't stare. Walking near dawn on summer mornings I often pass by cars and pickups parked along the old highway, hung over and half-dressed people stirring inside; people who most likely don't want to be seen, let alone greeted cheerfully in the light of dawn.

I don't care who they are; and even if I knew, I wouldn't tell. They might not believe that; this is a small town. But sex is a mystery, like faith, or love, and deserves to have the glow of silence around it.

I've been asked to preach this morning and am thinking about my sermon. The wind comes up with the dawn: two mule deer, a male and a female, cross the highway just a hundred feet in front of me, and run off into a hayfield. The wideness of God's mercy, as the old hymn says; the sudden way that grace makes all things good.

CAN YOU TELL THE TRUTH
IN A SMALL TOWN?

How do we tell the truth in a small town? Is it possible to write it? Certainly, great literature might come out of the lives of ordinary people on the farms and ranches and little towns of the Plains, but are the people who farm, the people working in those towns, writing it? The truth, the whole truth, tends to be complex, its contentments and joys wrestled out of doubt, pain, change. How to tell the truth in a small town, where, if a discouraging word is heard, it is not for public consumption?

Like many who have written about Dakota, I'm invigorated by the harsh beauty of the land and feel a need to tell the stories that come from its soil. Writing is a solitary act, and ideally, the Dakotas might seem to provide a writer with ample solitude and quiet. But the frantic social activity in small towns conspires to silence a person. There are far fewer people than jobs to fill. Someone must be found to lead the church choir or youth group, to bowl with the league, to coach a softball team or little league, to run a Chamber of Commerce or club committee. Many jobs are vital: the volunteer fire department and ambulance service, the domestic violence hotline, the food pantry. But all too often a kind of Tom Sawyerism takes over, and makes of adult life a perpetual club. Imagine spending the rest of your life at summer camp.

Women writers especially are in danger of being overwhelmed. As a rural North Dakota woman said to me at a writing workshop, "The world will continue to give more and more responsibility to any woman who will accept it." She had told friends she was at a meeting because she thought taking a writing workshop sounded frivolous. In Lemmon, it's possible for a woman to belong to one or more church groups, home extension club, Legion and hospital auxiliary, one or two women's clubs, bridge club, sewing club, country club, and several service club auxiliaries such as Jaycettes, each with their crafts projects, creeds, codes, and books of minutes, all of which read "a delicious lunch was served."

As one North Dakota writer says, "Here and there a woman has to step on a few toes and put her writing above other things." But in drawing back from the social whirl she sets herself apart from those around her, and in a small town this is hard to do. Someone who wants to write either has to break away or settle for writing only what is acceptable at a mother-daughter church banquet or a Girl Scout program.

Many writers depicting rural and small-town America, writers as diverse as Willa Cather, Sinclair Lewis, and Louise Erdrich, have found it necessary to write about that world from a distance. The distance may be mostly geographical, but it can also be the distance a profession provides: teaching in a college, for instance. In either case, the writer is insulated from the day-to-day realities of small-town or rural life. But a writer who is thoroughly immersed in Dakota's rural milieu, where nearly everyone is related, faces a particularly difficult form of self-censorship. "I'd like to write about my relatives," one North Dakota ranch woman told me, "but I'm no good at disguising things."

One popular form of writing on the Plains is the local history. These books reveal a great deal about the people who write them but do not often tell the true story of the region. In North Dakota, most homesteaders failed to remain on their land after proving up a claim, and the 1920s and 1930s brought farm bankruptcies and political upheaval, but you would never know it to read local histories, centered on those who made it. They present tales of perseverance made heroic in the context of the steady march of progress from homesteading days to the present. As one old-timer told me, "people have been writing it the way they wished it had been instead of the way it was."

The local history mentality that takes care not to offend the descendants of pioneer families who had grit enough to remain must, as anthropologist Seena Kohl says in an essay in *Plainswoman*, present the past "as a harmonious whole" that, despite its hardships, was preferable to the present. When this view of life comes off the page to dictate present reality, the consequences can be serious indeed. A fourth generation Dakotan, a high school student, wrote recently in a school theme that his family had always been here, and would always remain. "Always" in this context is less than seventy-five years, and with a fragile economy and a falling population, chances are this young man will have to seek his livelihood elsewhere. Having been raised for a world that does not exist, he may, sitting in an apartment in Minneapolis, Denver, or Spokane, come to see the Dakota prairie as a lost Eden. Maybe by the fifth generation the family will produce a writer who can excavate the story.

A more immediate consequence of the local history mentality is the tendency to "make nice." If we can make the past harmonious, why not the present? Why risk discussion that might cause unpleasantness? I was once at a pastor search

committee meeting when a woman said, "We don't want anyone too old." A pastor from a neighboring town who was
guiding us through the bureaucratic thickets, a woman who
had been ordained the week of her sixty-fifth birthday, said,
amicably but firmly, "I know most churches feel that way, but
maybe you should think about that." Another woman jumped
in and said, "Oh, we didn't mean anything. It was all in fun."

The bluntness of the first woman was at least useful: had she
been more urbane, she would have disguised her prejudice.
But the lie put forth by the other woman was intended to
silence us. Thanks to the minister's persistence, we did manage
a brief look at the question of what age we wanted our next
pastor to be, but it was painful. Among other things, it forced
us to look at the fact that our congregation is aging, and people
wanted to drop the subject as quickly as possible.

And what of truth? We don't tend to see the truth as something that could set us free because it means embracing pain,
acknowledging our differences and conflicts, taking our real
situation into account. Instead, in the isolated, insular small-
town and rural environment, truth itself can become an outside
authority, like the economic and political forces we profess
independence from, or the state and federal laws we so casually
break when they don't fit our needs. I am indebted to the
Reverend G. Keith Gunderson for this insight. He was vilified
not long ago by many in his town for protesting the custom of
allowing high school graduates to drink in the bars, no matter
what their age. The moral issue for him was not drinking but
respect for law. The reaction was mixed, but many felt that one
of their own — he was raised just thirty miles away — had
betrayed them. He should have known that this is simply how
we do things here.

A woman in another town baffled Medicaid fraud investigators when they discovered that she had been fudging figures for a local clinic, but with no personal gain in mind. It was just that the government had plenty of money and she knew how much we needed it. A typical small-town person in many ways, she saw herself as effectively dissociated from the law of the land. Anger over the incident was directed primarily at the professionals, doctors and clergy who cooperated in the government's investigation. Her friends and family never grasped that it was precisely their cooperation that kept the woman from going to jail.

It is a truism that outsiders, often professionals with no family ties, are never fully accepted into a rural or small-town community. Such communities are impenetrable for many reasons, not the least of which is the fact that the most important stories are never spoken of; the local history mentality has worn down their rough edges, or placed them safely out of sight, out of mind.

To learn the truth about the web of close-knit families that make up an isolated small town on the Plains, one must look back some years, to the men and women of the homesteading and early merchant generation. By now they've mostly been mythologized into the stern, hard-working papa and the over-worked-mother-who-never-complained, all their passions and complexities smoothed over. But many of these people, the women especially, had an intense love/hate relationship with the Plains that lives on in their children. Some mourned the loss of European culture or ethnic roots; others the social status they'd enjoyed in cities back East. Only the toughest survived here.

These women's ambivalence — or rage — toward the Plains

found expression in their relationships with their children; often they doted on the children who moved away while treating shabbily those who remained. The grandchildren growing up here developed, in self-defense, a world view in which everything from the outside world is suspect, while everything local, especially that which derives from the immediate family, is good. These are families that have an exceptionally difficult time dealing with conflict and change. Change means failure; it is a contaminant brought in by outside elements. Such families have brought the local history mentality to life, and in sufficient numbers they dictate the nature of their small towns. They are as precarious as they are deliberately, even obsessively, harmonious.

It is impossible to exaggerate how much the unconscious, the hidden story, dictates behavior in such families. If you know the story going back fifty years or so, their behavior makes sense. If you don't, and if you're an outsider, especially a teacher or pastor, someone whose profession connects with people's deepest (and most deeply embedded) needs, then God help you. You may wake one morning to find that all of the unresolved conflicts of lo these many generations have just been laid at your door.

And what if such a family produced a writer? How would it be possible to write the story, dig it out from the depths in which it is entombed? If truth has become an outside authority to be resisted in order to keep the family myths intact, then the writer seeking truth would have to become an outsider, too. This, in fact, is what often happens. One writer I know, a second generation North Dakotan who farms with her husband, was stunned to find, when she began a column in the weekly paper, that she suddenly felt insecure on her home turf.

She was surprised that so many of her friends reacted with a sullen silence, as if her column did not exist. "Something drives me to do this. I'm possessed to do this," she told me, "Maybe nothing drives them. Maybe it's a sin to be possessed in North Dakota."

Robert Kroetsch, a writer from the Canadian Plains, suggests that prairie writers can learn to see in "the particulars of place," old photographs, diaries, and the like, archaeological deposits of great value. But in my area more than one family has abandoned such evidence of their past; they've walked away from farmhouses and moved to town, leaving behind not only the oak furniture but old china and handmade quilts, even family photographs. The truth was so painful it literally had to be abandoned.

I wonder if the complex and often fragmented narrative style Kroetsch believes the prairie writer must adopt in "[trusting] to a version of archaeology" isn't squarely at odds with the local history mentality, which prefers a linear narrative, the progress model. I know from my experience working in a small-town library that writers like Larry Woiwode and Louise Erdrich are read warily by rural people on the Plains, if they are read at all. "Well, it's different," one woman said of *Love Medicine*, somewhat startled that the novel wasn't set in New York, Paris, or Hollywood, like a "real" best seller. "I didn't want anything like *this*," another woman said, returning *Beyond the Bedroom Wall;* "I just wanted a good story."

A good story is one that isn't demanding, that proceeds from A to B, and above all doesn't remind us of the bad times, the cardboard patches we used to wear in our shoes, the failed farms, the way people you love just up and die. It tells us instead that hard work and perseverance can overcome all obstacles; it tells lie after lie, and the happy ending is the happiest lie of all.

This is the reason why books like Woiwode's, or Richard Critchfield's *Those Days* or Lois Phillips Hudson's novel of the farm crisis of the 1920s, *The Bones of Plenty*, as relevant today as it ever was, tend to be buried by Plains people, cast down into the silence. Who wants to read Hudson's depiction of a farm wife's anguish over being torn from her roots, her home, her beloved piano: "If I go over and touch it now . . . just touch the middle C above the golden lock again, I would be turned into a pillar of salt; I would never have to walk out of here and get in the front seat of the car beside my husband, where the world says I belong."

Those times were hard enough to live through; there's no desire to read about them among people who raised their children to believe those hard times could never come again. Now that they're back, they and their children are doubly impoverished by having lost a native literature as well as the land homesteaded by their grandparents.

I write on the Plains, in a small town. I am indelibly an outsider, because I write and because I spent my formative years away. I am also an insider by virtue of family connections. I have a unique role here and try to respect its complexity. I have no family in the area now, but my roots go deep. When with considerable misgivings I joined my grandmother's Presbyterian church more than ten years after she died, an old woman startled me by saying, "It's good to have a Totten in the church again." People like her have helped recall me to my inheritance.

Not long ago I visited with a gentlemanly old cowboy in a tavern. He was in town, "buying provender," as he put it, and he sought me out as a member of what he termed "one of the old families," to tell me about a sidesaddle he owns that his great-grandfather made as a wedding present nearly 150 years ago. We mused a while on the subject of our ancestors, who traveled from many places — England, Scotland, Connecticut, Virginia, Iowa, Kansas — to settle on the Plains. Suddenly he said: "Who are we, and where do we come from? That's the real question, isn't it?" Before I could reply, he smiled slyly and said, "And here we are, telling each other lies." "Stories," I said, laughing. "Call them stories." "Stories?" he nearly shouted back. "That's who we are!" Slapping the bar, he repeated, *"Who we are!"*

Just a small moment, the philosophical enthusiasm of a tipsy but still courtly cowboy, but I think it reveals something about the sensitivity of Plains people to their past and present identities. I am entrusted with many stories here, and I have my own to tell. What I often wonder is why the others are not telling theirs. The material is certainly here: the economic upheavals of the last ten years alone might have inspired a novel as deeply Dakotan as *The Bones of Plenty*. Instead there is silence. We have comparatively few writers in the Dakotas, most of them teaching in our colleges or universities, which, as one of them, Jay Meek, has said, makes them "not *of* the [rural] communities, however much they might be *from* them." A few people in small towns write genre fiction — cowboy poetry, historical westerns, and the like — and some wonderful indigenous writing surfaces in memoirs and devotional literature, like a ranch woman's chronicle of the current farm crisis told through the Psalms, but mostly there is silence.

This is no doubt fine with many; artists are suspect in American society, as they bring uncomfortable truths to the surface.

But the silence here disturbs some who seek after truth; I've heard both clergy and board members of the North Dakota Arts Council wonder aloud what it means to have so few writers in the region. One minister told me he saw it as a kind of censorship, having a different cause than the censorship inflicted by totalitarianism or a military dictatorship, but with the same result. "I worry about us," he said, "if we aren't producing artists here who can tell our story. A people with no art has lost its soul."

Perhaps it will be another generation before the story of these days can be told. The children and grandchildren of farm people forced off their land today may well be the ones to write about it. Perhaps, given the distance that the passage of time can provide, they will give us back the truth about ourselves. Whether or not we will listen, out here on the Plains, I cannot say.

Weather Report: June 30

◆

I get started early, before six. It promises to be a good laundry day: a steady wind but not too strong. I come by my love of laundry honestly: my earliest memory is of my mother pulling clothes in from the sky on a line that ran out our apartment window in Washington, D.C.

Hanging up wet clothes while it is still cool, I think of her. Though she's lived in Honolulu for more than thirty years, she's a plainswoman at heart; her backyard clothesline is a dead giveaway. The challenge of drying clothes in a tropical valley agrees with her; mountain rains sweep down at least once a day, and she must be vigilant.

Here no rain is likely, unless, as so often happens, our most beautiful summer days turn dark and violent in late afternoon, thunderstorms pelting us with rain or hail. I think of a friend who was dying, who had saved up all her laundry for my visit. "I can't trust my husband with it," she whispered conspiratorially. "Men don't understand that clothes must be hung on a line."

She was right. Hanging up wet clothes gives me time alone under the sky to think, to grieve, and gathering the clean clothes in, smelling the sunlight on them, is victory.

GHOSTS
A History

In this place of which you say, "It is a waste" . . . there
shall be heard again the voice of mirth and the voice of
gladness, the voice of the bridegroom and the voice
of the bride, the voices of those who sing.
— *Isaiah 33:10–11*

THE CHURCH WAS MUSIC to me when I was little, an enthusiastic member of the cherub choir in the large Methodist church in Arlington, Virginia, where my dad was choir director. We wore pale blue robes with voluminous sleeves, stiff white collars, and floppy black bow ties, which I thought made me look like one of the angels in my picture hymnal.

I sang from that book every day at home. One of my strongest memories of early childhood is of sitting on my mother's lap at our old, battered Steinway upright as she played the hymns and I sang. By the time I was three, long before I knew how to read, I'd turn the pages and on seeing the illustration would begin singing the right song in the right pitch.

But music was no longer enough once I discovered the rosary owned by a Catholic friend in first grade. I decided I should have one too, and when my parents said I couldn't, I took an old necklace my mom had given me and said my own grace with it at the table, after family prayers. I had to mumble, because I had no idea what I was supposed to be saying.

This was too much for my father's Methodist blood. His grandfather had been a circuit rider in West Virginia and a chaplain in the Confederate Army. His father, my grandfather, had been a stonemason, lumberjack, and jug band banjo picker who got saved one night at a tent revival, worked his way through West Virginia Wesleyan, and spent the rest of his life preaching the Word. My dad said, ominously, that I could become a Catholic if I wanted to, but he also told me they had a list of books and movies I'd be forbidden to see. For the first time in my life I had come up against the idea that when something seems too good to be true, it probably is.

And this is who I am: a complete Protestant with a decidedly ecumenical bent. I never got that rosary when I was seven, but a friend gave me one when I'd been a Benedictine oblate for nearly five years. I still value music and story over systematic theology — an understatement, given the fact that I was so dreamy as a child that I learned not from Sunday school but from a movie on television that Jesus dies. Either my Sunday school teachers had been too nice to tell me (this was the 1950s), or, as usual, I wasn't paying attention. I am just now beginning to recognize the truth of my original vision: we go to church in order to sing, and theology is secondary.

I remember very little about my confirmation class in a Congregational church in Waukegan, Illinois, except that it was easy because I was good at memorizing, and the minister was a kindly man. I was still singing in my dad's choir, and music still seemed like the real reason for church. In high school in

Hawaii, my Methodist Youth Fellowship played volleyball with the Young Buddhist League.

My interest in religion deepened in adolescence, when my family joined a politically active United Church of Christ congregation, where adult classes were taught by professors of religion, one of them a German who had studied with Bultmann at Heidelberg. He was a good Lutheran, too; once, in his student days, he had a theological argument with his brother that got so bad the police had to be called.

I had a crush on him, and took a number of his classes, still totally innocent of both romance and theology; it's only with hindsight that I see I was on a disaster course. I was not yet a poet, but was destined to become one. I needed a teacher who would not have scorned Evelyn Underhill's *Mysticism*, a book I had found on my own, looking for some useful definition of religious experience. I needed liturgy and a solid grounding in the practice of prayer, not a demythologizing that left me feeling starved, thinking: If this is religion, I don't belong. Growing up and discovering who I was meant not going near a church again for nearly twenty years.

During that time I became a writer. I used to think that writing had substituted for religion in my life, but I've come to see that it has acted as a spiritual discipline, giving me the tools I needed to rediscover my religious heritage. It is my Christian inheritance that largely defines me, but for years I didn't know that.

In the early 1970s, when I was just out of college, working in New York City and hovering on the fringe of the Andy Warhol scene, a question crept into my consciousness one day, seemingly out of the blue: "What is sin?" I thought I should know, but my mind was blank. I felt like the little boy in *The Snow*

Queen who, as he's being carried off in the Queen's carriage, tries desperately to remember the Lord's Prayer but can think of nothing but the multiplication tables.

"What is sin?" It never occurred to me to go to a church for the answer. If the church hadn't taught me in my first twenty years what sin was, it probably never would. I now realize that the question was raised by the pious Protestant grandmother at my core. I had no idea she was there, and didn't know how to listen to her. I didn't realize it at the time, but my move in 1974 from New York to South Dakota was an attempt to hear her voice more clearly. It was a search for inheritance, for place. It was also a religious pilgrimage; on the ground of my grandmother's faith I would find both the means and the end of my search.

All of my grandparents lived out their faith on the Plains. My paternal grandparents, the Reverend John Luther Norris and his wife, Beatrice, served twelve Methodist churches in South Dakota and several more in Iowa. Prairie people have long memories, and they still tell stories about my grandfather's kindness. One man recalls that after his wife died, leaving him with several small children, he began drinking heavily. My grandfather came to his house one day to do the family's laundry, and though the man was drinking the whole time, my grandfather never preached about it; he just kept talking to him about his plans for the future, and, as he put it, "helped me straighten up my life." In his youth, my grandfather had been a black sheep in the Methodist fold, and he often exhibited more tolerance and flexibility than his wife, who clung to a rigid and often fierce fundamentalism.

My maternal grandfather, Frank Totten, was a doctor who practiced medicine in South Dakota for fifty-five years after moving from Kansas in 1909. He could be sentimental about religion but lacked faith; his wife, Charlotte, a former school-teacher, was a quietly pious Presbyterian, renowned in her church for the excellent Bible studies she conducted for the women's group. She was just about the only adult who could make me mind when I was little, and it was to her house that I moved in 1974, shortly after her death. I'm convinced that her spirit visited me in her kitchen and taught me how to bake bread using her bowl, her old wooden spoon and bread board. And for a time I tried on her Presbyterian church, the way I wore her old jackets and used her furniture. I still enjoyed singing hymns, but found that church was an uneasy exercise in nostalgia, and soon stopped going.

When some ten years later I began going to church again because I felt I needed to, I wasn't prepared for the pain. The services felt like word bombardment — agony for a poet — and often exhausted me so much I'd have to sleep for three or more hours afterward. Doctrinal language slammed many a door in my face, and I became frustrated when I couldn't glimpse the Word behind the words. Ironically, it was the language about Jesus Christ, meant to be most inviting, that made me feel most left out. Sometimes I'd give up, deciding that I just wasn't religious. This elicited an interesting comment from a pastor friend who said, "I don't know too many people who are so serious about religion they can't even go to church."

Even as I exemplified the pain and anger of a feminist looking warily at a religion that has so often used a male savior to keep women in their place, I was drawn to the strong old women in the congregation. Their well-worn Bibles said to me, "there is more here than you know," and made me take more seriously the religion that had caused my grandmother Totten's Bible to be so well used that its spine broke. I also began, slowly, to make sense of our gathering together on Sunday morning, recognizing, however dimly, that church is to be participated in and not consumed. The point is not what one gets out of it, but the worship of God; the service takes place both because of and despite the needs, strengths, and frailties of the people present. How else could it be? Now, on the occasions when I am able to actually worship in church, I am deeply grateful.

But the question of inheritance still haunts me, and I sometimes have the radical notion that I'm a Christian the way a Jew is a Jew, by maternal lineage. Flannery O'Connor remarks in her letters that "most of us come to the church by a means the church does not allow," and I may have put on my grandmother Totten's religion until it became my own. But the currents of this female inheritance spring from deep waters. Mary is also my ancestor, as is Eve. As Emily Dickinson once said, "You know there is no account of her death in the Bible, and why am I not Eve?" Or, why not my two grandmothers, reflecting two very different strains of American Protestantism that exist in me as a continual tension between curse and blessing, pietism and piety, law and grace, the God of wrath and the God of love.

When I was very small my fundamentalist grandmother Norris, meaning well, told me about the personal experience I'd have with Jesus one day. She talked about Jesus coming and the world ending. It sounded a lot like a fairy tale when the prince comes, only scarier. Fundamentalism is about control more than grace, and in effect my grandmother implanted the seed of fundamentalism within me, a shadow in Jungian terms, that has been difficult to overcome. Among other things, it made of Christological language a stumbling block, and told me that as a feminist, as a thinking and questioning person, I had no business being in church. More insidiously, it imbedded in me an unconscious belief in a Monster God. For most of my life you could not have convinced me that, to quote a Quaker friend, "trust comes before belief and faith is a response to love more than an acceptance of dogma."

Trust is something abused children lack, and children raised with a Monster God inside them have a hard time regaining it. My uncle told me once about having his mother sit at the edge of his bed and tell him that Jesus might come as a thief in the night and tomorrow could be that great day when the world ends. "That sucks when you'd been planning a ball game and a rubber gun battle," he said. He would pull the covers over his head when she left, and try to shut out the sounds of Jesus sneaking around in the dark.

A few years ago when I was on retreat at a monastery a poem came boiling up out of me. Called "The Jesus They Made For Us," it is an exorcism of the Monster God:

> He was a boy who drank his mother's milk
> He was always kind to children
> He swallowed them like fish
> He drank up all his mother's milk
> He ate up stars like candy
> He swallowed the sea like a hungry whale

This last image came from a dream I'd had in which I lay on a beach unable to move as a giant whale swam toward me, meaning to rape and crush me. I suspected that this whale was my true image of God, a legacy of my childhood.

A few days later I happened to visit with a little girl who showed me her drawing journal. A recent entry was a big blue

whale with three words printed underneath it in purple cray-
on: "God Is Love." Startled, I said, "That's a wonderful picture," and she replied dreamily, "I just love that whale." With
no small sense of awe I realized that we had each partaken of a
powerful image, and the difference in how we perceived it
amounted to the difference between us. This taught me a new
appreciation of what it means to approach the holy as a little
child, and some of my trust was restored.

But trust in the religious sphere has been hard to come by.
Like many Americans of my baby boom generation, I had
thought that religion was a constraint that I had overcome by
dint of reason, learning, artistic creativity, sexual liberation.
Church was for little kids or grandmas, a small-town phenom-
enon that one grew out of or left behind. It was a shock to
realize that, to paraphrase Paul Simon, all the crap I learned in
Sunday school was still alive and kicking inside me. I was also
astonished to discover how ignorant I was about my own religion. Apart from a few Bible stories and hymns remembered
from childhood I had little with which to start to build a mature
faith. I was still that child in *The Snow Queen*, asking "what is
sin?" but not knowing how to find out. Fortunately a Benedictine friend provided one answer: "Sin, in the New Testament,"
he told me, "is the failure to do concrete acts of love." That is
something I can live with, a guide in my conversion. It's also a
much better definition of sin than I learned as a child: sin as
breaking rules.

Comprehensible, sensible sin is one of the unexpected gifts
I've found in the monastic tradition. The fourth-century monks
began to answer a question for me that the human potential
movement of the late twentieth century never seemed to address: if I'm O.K. and you're O.K., and our friends (nice people

and, like us, markedly middle class, if a bit bohemian) are O.K., why is the world definitely not O.K.? Blaming others wouldn't do. Only when I began to see the world's ills mirrored in myself did I begin to find an answer; only as I began to address that uncomfortable word, sin, did I see that I was not being handed a load of needless guilt so much as a useful tool for confronting the negative side of human behavior.

The desert monks were not moralists concerned that others behave in a proper way so much as people acutely aware of their own weaknesses who tried to see their situation clearly without the distortions of pride, ambition, or anger. They saw sin (what they called bad thoughts) as any impulse that leads us away from paying full attention to who and what we are and what we're doing; any thought or act that interferes with our ability to love God and neighbor. Many desert stories speak of judgment as the worst obstacle for a monk. "Abba Joseph said to Abba Pastor: 'Tell me how I can become a monk.' The elder replied: 'If you want to have rest here in this life and also in the next, in every conflict with another say, "Who am I?" and judge no one.' "

One of my favorite monastic stories in this regard concerns a desert monk who is surprised to hear that a gardener in a nearby city has a way of life more pleasing to God than his own. Visiting the city he finds the man selling vegetables, and asks for shelter overnight. The gardener, overcome with joy to be of service, welcomes the monk into his home. While the monk admires the gardener's hospitality and life of prayer, he is disturbed to find that the vulgar songs of drunks can be heard coming from the street, and asks the gardener: "Tell me, what do you conceive in your heart when you hear these things?" The man replies, "That they are all going to the kingdom." The old monk marvels and says, "This is the practice which surpasses my labor of all these years. Forgive me, brother, I have not yet approached this standard." And without eating, he withdraws again into the desert.

The monk, as virtuous as he is, recognizes that he has room for improvement. Chances are he would agree with Gregory of Nyssa, a fourth-century theologian, that sin is the failure to grow. In our own century, Carl Jung has reminded us that to grow we must eventually stop running from our "shadow" and turn to face it. Around the time I joined my grandmother's church I dreamed that a fundamentalist minister and his flock had surrounded my house, threatening to bury me alive under a truckload of rocks and dirt. I sat inside, feeling helpless as they sang hymns and shouted curses. Finally, however, I went outside to face them. I ordered them to leave, and woke up feeling as if a great weight had been lifted from me.

I realized just how far I'd come later that year in a writing workshop. One student was a Pentecostal Christian who wrote testimonies, and early one morning I wept as I read one. It could have been my grandmother Norris speaking and it frightened me for that reason, but her work was also in need of editing and I had a terrific responsibility, as the woman had never before submitted any writing for criticism. Fortunately, she took to editing like a duck to water, but what moved me deeply was her thanking me for being open to the religious nature of her work.

Religion is in my blood, and in my ghosts. My maternal grandmother Totten had a livable faith and a tolerance that allowed her to be open to the world. My grandmother Norris lived with the burden of a harder faith. She had married my grandfather — a divorced man whose wife had abandoned him and their two small children — after his conversion at a revival meeting. The older sister she revered became a medical missionary, but my grandmother found her mission in marriage and in raising seven children as the wife of a Plains pastor who served in seventeen churches in thirty-two years. Their first child born on the Plains, Kathleen Dakota, was born with rickets. While my grandmother was still nursing she conceived again; her doctor found her too exhausted and malnourished to sustain another pregnancy and performed an abortion. Early in their marriage her husband had rejected her affection in such a way that it was still fresh in her memory sixty years later. Long after he was dead she could calmly say, "You know, of course, he never loved me."

Her last child was born when she was in her forties, soon after her stepson, the eldest, died of meningitis. She prayed for another boy and promised the Lord that she would rear him to become a minister if her prayers were answered — Grandma Norris was nothing if not biblical. She had a son who tried and failed to live out her plans for him; only years later did she affirm him in his chosen vocation of teaching, reasoning that Jesus was a teacher, too. For most of her life she would ask of anyone she met: "Are you saved?"

It's this hard religion, adding fuel to an all-American mix of incest, rape, madness, and suicide, that nearly destroyed an entire generation in my family. My father's status as oldest remaining son, his musical talent, a sense of humor, and a solid marriage helped save him. But my aunts suffered terribly, and one was lost. I never met her; she died the year I was born. She died of lots of things: sex and fundamentalist religion and schizophrenia and postpartum despair. She was a good girl who became pregnant out of wedlock and could make no room for the bad girl in herself. She jumped out of a window at a state mental hospital a few days after she had her baby.

Looking at an old family photograph when I was twelve, I saw a face I didn't recognize. Asking who this was, I first heard her story. Suicides have a way of haunting the next generation, and adolescence is when most of us begin to know who we will be. I believe I became a writer in order to tell her story and possibly redeem it. This goes much deeper than anything I understand but, in part, I also joined a church because of her. I needed to find that woman sacrificed to a savage god. I needed to make sure she was forgiven and at peace.

The first time I stayed at a monastery hermitage I surfaced one day for morning prayer with the community. My stomach was growling, anticipating breakfast, and I was restless. A monk read what I've since learned is a prayer they say every morning, that all their deceased confreres, oblates, relatives, benefactors, and friends may rest in the peace of the risen Christ. That morning, I knew it was done; I didn't have to worry about my aunt any more. They tell me this is Catholic theology, not Protestant; I couldn't care less. Her name was Mary, and she had good pitch. The church was music to her, and she sang all her life in church choirs.

EVIDENCE OF FAILURE

M Y GRANDMOTHER TOTTEN'S RAINBARREL, tipped on its side. She would draw water from it to rinse her hair; she would fill a dented sprinkler can to water her houseplants and flower garden. I let water freeze in it and the bottom buckled.

The lily of the valley in her flower bed that I never rescued from weeds whose names I don't know.

The piano gathering dust in my living room.

Standing in the weeds around the auctioneer's truck: a bird's-eye maple bedroom set, a vanity with oval mirror, a bed with a scrolled headboard, a dainty desk and straight-backed chair. Some dry rot. Sold: one hundred dollars.

Three houses on a farm tucked into the folds of the Grand River breaks: a stone house, a log cabin, a two-story frame with gabled roof. Each built with care, each placed farther above flood stage, each built bigger to accommodate a growing family. Abandoned now, a patchwork quilt still on the attic bed, a well-worn whetstone by the kitchen door.

The graves of two small boys, two of many who died in the influenza epidemics of the early 1920s; Doc Totten's sons.

A Bible inscribed, *Dr. Mrs. Totten*, its back broken, the binding glue dried out and the webbing on its spine exposed: prayers clipped from newspapers tucked throughout its pages, the yellowed paper crumbling. A handwritten prayer, "Keep me friendly to myself, keep me gentle in disappointment," has weathered badly in the long crescendo of Romans 8. And in the Psalms, a dried prairie rose, a photograph of a baby in a coffin.

A brochure printed on cheap green paper announcing "John Luther Norris, Evangelist, a man whose heart is warm with the Gospel." He tried to save Deadwood in 1924.

Shadows 'n' Owls:
A Message from Jim Sullivan

———◆———

Dairy farming made an empiricist out of me. When I was a little boy I had to walk alone at night with bucket and lantern, down through the trees by the river, and milk cows in a dark barn. There was no room in my life for bogeymen or poltergeists, anything I couldn't explain. There were shadows 'n' owls, that's all.

CANA

LIVING IN A TOWN SO SMALL that, as one friend puts it, the poets and ministers have to hang out together has its advantages. We raid each other's libraries and sustain decent arguments on matters of science, politics, and religion.

Once a clergyman dropped by as we were finishing dinner with two other friends, a sheep rancher and a bridge crew foreman for the Burlington Northern. Discussion turned to Ockham's razor, the medieval antecedent of modern empiricism, which states that given a choice of explanations of phenomena, one should choose the most simple.

"I don't believe in metaphysics," my husband said. The pastor replied, "I don't believe in Ockham's razor." At this Jim, the bridge foreman, struck his forehead in dismay, saying, "See what biblical studies will *do* to a person!"

There is wariness on both sides: poets and Christians have been at odds with one another, off and on, for two thousand years. There is also trust: we are people who believe in the power of words to effect change in the human heart.

I'm at a hermitage in high summer. At four this morning a bird began singing in the grove; within an hour he had raised a chorus. The wind comes up, then suddenly is still, in the green flame that is this world.

An orange butterfly lights on my arm. The abbey bells begin to ring. I had resisted coming here, but a clergy friend said: "You'll go to the monastery, pull yourself together, and write it out."

"You don't know what you're asking," I snapped. He said: "That's what Jesus said to his mother at Cana."

WHERE I AM

When you get the feeling that the whole world can see
you but no one is watching, you have come to the
grasslands of North America.
— DAN O'BRIEN, *In the Center of the Nation*

WHERE I AM IS America's outback, the grasslands west of
the 100th meridian that constitute the western half of North
and South Dakota, Nebraska, Kansas, Oklahoma, and Texas.
In all that vast space, extending all the way to the 107th meridian in eastern Montana and Wyoming, there are far more cattle
than people. Only two cities (Lubbock and Amarillo) have
populations of over 100,000, and there is only one large university, Texas Tech. Where I am is a town of 1,600 people that
is by far the largest in northwestern South Dakota, an area
encompassing nearly 15,000 square miles in seven counties,
roughly the size of Delaware, New Jersey, Connecticut, and
Rhode Island combined.

Where I am is a marginal place that is at the very center of
North America, roughly 1,500 miles from the Atlantic and
Pacific oceans, the Gulf of Mexico, and the Arctic Archipelago.
It's a land of extremes, holding the absolute temperature range
record for the Western Hemisphere, set in 1936 when a town in
western North Dakota registered temperatures from 60 degrees
below zero to 121 above within the same year.

Where I am is the West River of Dakota, a plateau that rises sharply out of the narrow valley of the Missouri River and extends to the Rocky Mountains. It's a high plains desert, full of sage and tumbleweed and hardy shortgrass, where it rains fifteen inches in a good year (New York City averages 44; Chicago, 33; San Francisco, 20) but is often as dry as Los Angeles, with an annual rainfall of only twelve inches. In a bad drought we register precipitation that is more like that of Phoenix, just seven inches a year.

It's a place where a pleasantly warm summer day with clear skies often means a violent thunderstorm with hail by late afternoon, where my enjoyment of the perennials in my garden is tempered by the knowledge that the ground they're in will be frozen hard for at least four months.

Where I am is a place that does not readily render its secrets or subtleties. Standing on a hillside near the Grand River in central Perkins County, you realize suddenly that you are on the highest ground for many miles around, and that the stones nearby are not random but were placed there by human hands long ago. They are teepee rings, and this is a lookout site for buffalo. You notice patches of deep green in a shallow draw and realize that they are ruts from the old trail to Seim, now drowned under a manmade lake, a former stop on the stagecoach route between Fort Lincoln near Mandan, North Dakota, and the Black Hills.

Where I am is a place where Native Americans and whites live alone together, to paraphrase David Allen Evans, a South Dakota poet. Many small towns are Indian or white, and in general there is a deafening silence between the two worlds, a silence exacerbated by ignorance and intolerance on both sides. Many in the dominant white culture seem content with an indifference that amounts to "live and let die," given the drastic unemployment and low life expectancy in the impoverished Indian community.

Signs of hope are few. Chuck Woodard, an English professor at South Dakota State University, sees a possibility for change in a new curriculum currently being developed for public school students in grades K–12. "My hopes are based on the initially positive responses from people to this new curriculum," he says. "My fears are based on past history, a history of the short-term enthusiasms of American society."

I find hope each year at Prairie Winds, a three-day writing workshop for high school students and their teachers held annually in the Black Hills. A good third of the participants are Native American, and this provides an unusual opportunity for Indians and whites to meet in a reflective environment with no issues to contend with beyond the commitment to writing.

I'll never forget the year that my group consisted of six girls, three Lakota and three white. At our first meeting the white girls, all precociously verbal, wouldn't shut up, and the Lakota girls wouldn't speak. Everyone was nervous, including me. Knowing that silence is typically Sioux — a virtue, as well as a common reaction to a new and possibly threatening social situation dominated by whites — I decided in desperation to have us "make silence," a trick I had learned from the Benedictines.

We arranged our chairs in a circle and held hands. I had to resort to counting to three in order to begin the silence, one girl literally having to swallow the end of a sentence. And we kept the silence for over a minute, during which time shy smiles began darting around the circle. By the time we finished we were relaxed enough to take turns speaking; we were better able to listen to one another. The shyest of the Lakota girls didn't say anything until the next day, but it was understood that this was all right.

We found that we liked our silence and kept coming back to it. We liked the way it made a space for us in the midst of noise — a teenager cursing a computer printer, construction workers hammering in an addition to the lodge — and the way it allowed friendships to develop. We began to talk about our real lives, and even talked about how unusual it was, in South Dakota, for whites and Indians to meet like this, to be human together.

Where I am is a place where the human fabric is worn thin, farms and ranches and little towns scattered over miles of seemingly endless, empty grassland. On a clear night you can see not only thousands of stars but the lights of towns fifty miles away. Scattered between you and the horizon, the lights of farmhouses look like ships at sea. The naturalist Loren Eiseley once commented on the way Plains people "have been strung out at nighttime under a vast solitude rather than linked to the old-world village with its adjoining plots. We were mad to settle the West in [this] fashion," he says. "You cannot fight the sky." But some have come to love living under its winds and storms. Some have come to prefer the treelessness and isolation, becoming monks of the land, knowing that its loneliness is an honest reflection of the essential human loneliness. The willingly embraced desert fosters realism, not despair.

I'm tempted to despair at times. For one thing, Dakota can be painfully lonely for the artist, and it's as hard for us to make a living here as it is for any farmer or rancher. Our difference stands out in an area where quiet conformity is the norm, and sometimes our local friends ask David and me, "Don't you ever miss having people to talk to about what you do?" The answer is yes, and no. A fledgling ascetic, I am learning to see loneliness as a seed that, when planted deep enough, can grow into writing that goes back out into the world. I'm also developing an ascetic's keen appreciation for the gifts of fast and feast. On the rare occasions when my writing engenders response and I'm invited to go play poet for a day or two at a college, it does seem like a feast.

And, on occasion, other artists come to me. Once a modern dance troupe came to Lemmon to work in the schools. They choreographed a witty dance about tilling the soil and got high school students to perform it. They held a workshop for the football team on avoiding injury and working with damaged muscles. They asked me to participate in a collaboration of dance and poetry, something I'd never done, although I know many dancers from my days at Bennington.

Best of all, the troupe managed to assault a number of racial and social stereotypes held by the young people of Lemmon, whose knowledge of the outer world is severely limited. Much of what they know of other races they get from television cop shows. One dancer was a black man who had been raised on a farm in Indiana and had broken horses for a living. He'd been a bull rider on the rodeo circuit and told the students he'd given it up because it wasn't good for his body. "I'd rather dance," he said, and I felt he'd earned his fee right there.

Out of gratitude I fed the dancers rich, carbohydrate-laden meals for three nights running. One evening after supper was over and the table had been cleared, we sat drinking coffee and began to talk about feet. One dancer, to illustrate a point, took off her socks and shoes and placed a foot on the table. Soon we had all followed suit, and as we talked I realized that we had, by this odd gesture, stumbled into community. Dance, after all, is a communal affair, and we had just made a community of those willing to bare the lowly foot. It was hospitality, an exchange of gifts, that had brought this about; the dancers' giving of themselves all week in teaching and performing, and my feeding them as they needed to be fed.

Hospitality is of primary importance in the desert. Bedouin hospitality is legendary, as is that of the Benedictines, who are instructed by Saint Benedict in his *Rule* to "receive all guests as Christ." The people of the Great Plains can be hospitable as well, in the fashion of people who have little and are willing to share what they have. The poorest among us, in the Native American community, are exceptional in this regard, with a tradition of hospitality that has deep cultural roots in the giveaway, a sacred event that in application served the purpose of providing for the entire tribe. Hunters brought their surplus meat or buffalo robes, and those too old or infirm to hunt brought handcrafted items like quillwork; and in the exchange everyone received what was needed to survive the winter. Even today the ceremonial giveaway, in the words of Arthur Amiotte, a Lakota artist, remains an important and "reciprocal activity in which we are reminded of sacred principles," an act of giving which "ennobles the human spirit."

Visitors from urban areas are often surprised by the easy friendliness they encounter on the Plains. Even in Bismarck-Mandan (at 64,000, a major urban area by Dakota standards) strangers greet travelers on the street and welcome them warmly. Recently a motel manager drove a woman nearly two hundred miles to the town where her husband had fallen ill, and stayed with her until family arrived. This could happen in a larger city, of course, but it's the expected thing on the Plains.

Like all desert hospitality, this is in part a response to the severity of the climate; here, more demonstrably than in many other places, we need each other to survive.

But hospitality to the stranger does not necessarily translate into greater love for the people you live with every day, and the small town of both the heartland and the monastery are often stereotyped as either paradise on earth or backwaters full of provincial and self-righteous hypocrites. The truth, as is so often the case, lies somewhere in between.

I have observed that in the small town, the need to get along favors the passive aggressives, those for whom honest differences and disagreements pose such a threat that they are quickly submerged, left to fester in a complex web of resentments. This is why, when the tempests erupt in the small-town teapot, they are so violently destructive. This is why, when the comfortable fiction that we're all the same under the skin, is exposed as a lie, those who are genuinely different so often feel ostracized and eventually leave.

The monasteries I am familiar with in Dakota also have their problems, the small-town problems of personality clashes at close quarters, of gossip, of pigeonholing people or taking them for granted. But overall they seem healthier than the towns. Benedictines live in such close proximity, and in his *Rule* Saint Benedict so clearly takes into account the different personalities and needs of individuals that one doesn't get far by pretending that everyone is the same; the monastery is far less likely than the small town to end up with conformity at the expense of community.

I'm not sure that Benedictines get along any better on average than small-town people do, but observation has led me to think that the fear of controversy that often paralyzes the small-town gathering, ensuring its dullness, is less a factor in the monastery, where scripture and the liturgy act as a leaven enabling (and sometimes forcing) people to be less defensive and fearful of one another. An example of how a monastic community and a small-town women's church group dealt with controversy will serve to illustrate this point.

A Benedictine sister from the Philippines once told me what her community did when some sisters took to the streets in the popular revolt against the Marcos regime. Some did not think it proper for nuns to demonstrate in public, let alone risk arrest. In a group meeting that began and ended with prayer, the sisters who wished to continue demonstrating explained that this was for them a religious obligation; those who disapproved also had their say. Everyone spoke; everyone heard and gave counsel.

It was eventually decided that the nuns who were demonstrating should continue to do so; those who wished to express solidarity but were unable to march would prepare food and provide medical assistance to the demonstrators, and those who disapproved would pray for everyone. The sister laughed and said, "If one of the conservative sisters was praying that we young, crazy ones would come to our senses and stay off the streets, that was O.K. We were still a community."

Things were different at a meeting of a church women's group in a small Dakota town, when a younger member distributed informational pamphlets about an upcoming election. Prepared by the county agricultural extension service, they explained in a nonpartisan manner several complicated constitutional issues on the state ballot. The woman was stunned to discover a few days later that another woman, a former teacher, had been criticizing her behind her back for bringing politics to the women's Bible circle. This is a story about fear, a fear so pervasive that even in a small group of people you've known most of your life you can't speak up, you can't risk talking about issues. That meeting had begun and ended with prayer, but no one had a say, no one was heard, and community was diminished.

Paradoxically, though monks are said to be "formed" into one way of life, monasteries are full of people who feel free to be themselves, often to the point of eccentricity. (An abbot once said to me, "if there is any such thing as a 'typical' monk, we sure don't have any here.") A monastery is cohesive; it is not a schismatic society that survives by expelling those who don't fit into a mold. This difference might be summed up in two versions of heaven I once heard from a Benedictine nun: in one, heaven is full of people you love, and in the other, heaven is where you love everyone who is there.

I once heard a woman in my church refuse outright to accept the help of another woman whose talents we could have used in presenting a musical program. It was rare to receive such an offer of help, and I thought it a shame to reject it and risk rejecting the woman in the process. But a personality clash or bad experience in the past had led this person to say, angrily and with grim finality: "I won't work with her." I couldn't help wishing we were in a monastery, where an abbot or prioress could command us under obedience to work with that woman, and maybe grow in our understanding of what Christian charity, and community, demand.

One thing that distinguishes the monastery from the small town is that the *Rule* of Saint Benedict, read aloud daily and constantly interpreted, provides definition of certain agreed-upon values that make for community. The small-town minister, expected to fill the role of such a rule by reminding people to love one another, is usually less effectual.

Benedict's admonishment to "bear with the greatest patience the infirmities of others," often acts like fresh air blowing into what could be the ultimate closed system, the smallest small town. Benedict was well aware that, as he put it, "thorns of contention are likely to spring up" in communal living, and he recommends as a remedy reciting the Lord's Prayer at both morning and evening office each day. "Thus warned by the pledge they make to one another in the very words of this prayer: *Forgive us as we forgive*," he writes, the monks may "cleanse themselves of this kind of vice."

It seems to work. As one monk told me, "When someone in the community is driving me up the wall, we are still in church together four times a day. And that begins to make a difference. It takes the edge off." When I hear one monk complaining about another, however harsh the remark, however acute the exasperation or even rage, I sense that I am hearing an honest acknowledgment of differences grounded in love. Monks, after all, are conscious of moving, as Benedict says, "together unto life everlasting."

This might help explain the incredible expansiveness of Benedictine hospitality that on more than one occasion has turned my Dakota desert into a garden. One event could only have happened on the Plains, where monasteries are not besieged by many guests. I was visiting over Palm Sunday and the monk in charge of liturgy asked if I would take the part of one of the Gospel readers, the servant girl who nails Peter. I accepted, but scarcely felt I belonged; my being in church at all seemed unreal, either great folly or a miracle of hospitality on the part of both God and the monks. Later that day I read a vision of Mechtild of Magdeburg, a fiery and controversial mystic of the thirteenth century who was taken in by the Benedictines in her old age. I felt a twinge of recognition in her description of herself as someone who did not feel at home in church. As Mechtild was often in trouble with ecclesiastical authorities who frequently denied her the sacraments, this has a special poignancy. But in her vision the Blessed Virgin herself invites Mechtild into the choir, to "stand in front of Saint Catherine."

I sat in front of the abbey's farm manager, not Saint Catherine, but small difference. This is the power of desert hospitality: it transcends all our categories of division — male/female, Catholic/Protestant, celibate/married, monk/layperson — and changes us in the process.

Esther de Waal, a student of Benedictine spirituality, has described the Christian life as a series of open doors, and while I know that this is incomprehensible to many people, it is true of my experience in the monastery. After Mass that Palm Sunday, I wept for joy in my room, but I also laughed aloud when I read of Mechtild that "theology was not her strong point." To use a modern idiom, I could relate to that. For me, the greatest gift of the monastic tradition, beginning with the desert stories that contain some of the best theology I know, and continuing with my own experience of the Benedictines, is how easily and even beautifully theology converts into experience, and vice versa. It's a boon of the monastic liturgy, something I happen to have discovered in the desert of a monastery on the high plains desert of Dakota, and now no longer wish to live without.

The West River of Dakota encourages you to either make or

find deserts for yourself. Sometimes it's a matter of adjusting to a harsh climate. (I'm writing this in a hermitage where the temperature by 11:30 A.M. is 92 degrees; the old air conditioner works, but drowns out the sound of birds and wind, so I don't use it.) Sometimes it means suffering in the constricted social atmosphere of a small town or seeking out the disciplined routine of a monastery. But in all of these places that couldn't be more deprived by worldly standards I also find an expansiveness, a giddy openness that has allowed me to discover gifts in myself and others that most likely would have remained hidden in more busy, sophisticated, or luxuriant surroundings.

In the small town on the Plains, as in the monastery, there are so few people for so many jobs that we tend to call on whoever seems the most likely to do the job well. This has its bad side, as capable people can find that they are doing too much. It can also lead to mediocrity. Many local events have made me think of what Minnesota writer Carol Bly has suggested as a motto for small towns: "If a thing is worth doing, it's worth doing badly."

But sometimes miracles occur. Sometimes people rise to the occasion and do well more than they believe they can do at all. The radical hope we must place in others on the Plains reminds me of Jesus, who called disciples from their ordinary work to change the world without once consulting a personnel manager to determine if they had the aptitude or credentials for the job.

When the pastor of our Presbyterian church in Lemmon moved away a few years ago, we were left with the task of filling the pulpit for an indeterminate period. The chair of the worship committee immediately commandeered me to preach, saying simply, "You're a writer, you can do it." And, to my surprise, I did. I had to confront some family ghosts, among them the fierce Methodist preachers in my blood. I had to contend with my own uncertain Christian faith. But the need was there, and I was able to answer it, preaching well enough so that in effect I became our half-time pastor for eight months, until other duties called me away.

There were other surprises in store for the congregation; we found that one of our elders, a housewife and proud of it, could lead a very dignified communion service. She also preached several fine devotional sermons, one on the subject of housework. What good is a desert? Well, I believe a desert is where such gifts appear. In a larger urban church with well-credentialed clergy, that woman and I would not have been asked to preach. We would never have discovered that we could preach. But on the Plains, as in the desert, book learning and training matters less than one's ability to draw from the well of one's experience, to learn by doing (a motto of John Dewey's). It's also a founding principle of Bennington College, and it amuses me to find that I'm finally living it nearly thirty years after graduation and a world away.

The aging congregations in small towns on the Plains may be an endangered species. But so are the family farmers of Dakota, and Benedictine monks, for that matter. All are generally viewed by the rest of the world as irrelevant or anachronistic. And yet we may find important lessons in these overlooked and undervalued lives. Despite their dwindling numbers, and despite the fact that they, like the rest of us, so often fail at caring for one another as they should, churchgoers are trying to keep alive both hope and community values.

Small-town churchgoers are often labeled hypocrites, and sometimes they are. But maybe they are also people who have learned to live with imperfection, what Archbishop Rembert Weakland, a Benedictine, recently described as "the new asceticism." Living with people at close range over many years, as both monastics and small-town people do, is much more difficult than wearing a hair shirt. More difficult, too, I would add, than holding to the pleasant but unrealistic ideal of human perfectibility that seems to permeate much New Age thinking.

And there is the land. Family farmers and monks cultivate living lightly on the land, the farmers because they love it and want to preserve it for their children, the Benedictines because their communities put down permanent roots. Neither are frontier people in the exploitative sense of the word — those who take all there is from a place and then move on. As it becomes increasingly obvious that the human race will eventually run out of places to move on to, their wisdom and way of life may prove important to all of us.

Many people are just waking to the reality that unlimited expansion, what we call progress, is not possible in this world, and maybe looking to monks (who seek to live within limitations) as well as rural Dakotans (whose limitations are forced upon them by isolation and a harsh climate) can teach us how to live more realistically. These unlikely people might also help us overcome the pathological fear of death and the inability to deal with sickness and old age that plague American society.

Consumerism is fed by a desire to forget our mortality. But Benedict instructs his monks to remind themselves every day that they are going to die, and in Dakota death has an undeniable day-to-day reality. The brutal massacres of Wounded Knee and the Killdeer Mountains (misnamed a "battle" to this day) are too recent to be comfortably relegated to history; they're still a living memory for the Native American community. And for white settlers, the period since the end of the "Indian Wars" has been marked by the slow death of their towns, churches, schools, and way of life. We learn to live with a hard reality: nothing lasts. As a pastor friend who has served in the Dakotas for nearly thirty years recently wrote to me, "Dakota civilization does not support the idea that institutions will live on and we with them . . . quite possibly what we value so highly might not even outlast us."

Maybe the desert wisdom of the Dakotas can teach us to love anyway, to love what is dying, in the face of death, and not pretend that things are other than they are. The irony and wonder of all this is that it is the desert's grimness, its stillness and isolation, that bring us back to love. Here we discover the paradox of the contemplative life, that the desert of solitude can be the school where we learn to love others.

In the monastic tradition, the desert of deprivation and solitude has always been the well-spring of self-giving love. A scholar of the early Christian church, Peter Brown captured the essence of this paradox in writing about Anthony, one of the earliest of the desert ascetics, considered to have set the tone for the monastic movement in Christendom. Brown points out that the battle for the heart is the one that mattered to Anthony far more than the battle for control of his bodily desires. He writes that the message of Anthony's life, that later monks made into a model of monasticism, was

revealed (in Anthony's last years) ever more frequently in the quintessentially fourth-century gift of sociability. He came to radiate such magnetic charm, and openness to all, that any stranger who came upon him, surrounded by crowds of disciples, visiting monks, and lay pilgrims, would know at once, in that dense press of black-garbed figures, which one was the great Anthony. He was instantly recognizable as someone whose heart had achieved total transparency to others.

I have seen that transparency in a few old monks who over many years have come to incarnate hospitality. This doesn't seem like something one could aspire to, but it's inspiring to see how much ordinary human defensiveness can wear away in a well-lived and holy life. My own life has opened up more than I thought possible in the Dakota desert, the desert of the monastery and of the small town, the desert of a small and fairly conservative Presbyterian church.

I believe that it is because they so consciously and willingly live out the paradox of the desert that the monastic communities on the high Plains are more open to change than the small towns here, and are therefore more likely to survive. It is partly that monastic people value the leaven that outsiders can bring: as they're not easily suckered by the all-American myth of self-reliance and self-sufficiency, they're less likely to persist in thinking they can stand alone. Monks are also less likely to hide like mushrooms, like some small-town people I know who suffer in silent and obsessive despair as the inevitable happens, and another family moves out of town, eroding the tax base, putting on the market another house that won't find a buyer.

For one who has chosen the desert and truly embraced the forsaken ground it is not despair or fear or limitation that dictates how one lives. One finds instead an openness and hope that verges on the wild: ◆

Abbot Lot went to see Abbot Joseph and said: "Father, according as I am able, I keep my little rule, and my little fast, my prayer, meditation and contemplative silence; and according as I am able I strive to cleanse my heart of bad thoughts: now what more should I do?" The elder rose up in reply and stretched out his hands to heaven, and his fingers became like lamps of fire. He said: "why not become all flame?"

STAR-TIME

W<small>E'RE IN THE MIDDLE OF A CYCLONE</small>," said an old monk as I watched with him and most of the community at dusk, as sheet upon sheet of rain marched toward the refectory windows, then spun off in the opposite direction. The wind came first from the north, then the south, as cold air pushed the day's heat upward. All became heavy and still. Lightning took out the monastery phones. ("A blessing," said one monk, "peace at last.") Then a hard rain came and lasted about an hour.

In yesterday's storm the land itself seemed to race along under low, fast clouds. Today the land is still, as if waiting for the Magritte clouds painted on the bright blue sky to move.

By early afternoon the muddy road has turned to dust. I am on an ancient sea bed, the edge of the unglaciated Missouri plateau, looking at prehistory. The forty miles of moraine unfolding before me was carried by a glacier long before the Wisconsin ice sheet covered eastern Dakota.

Walking downhill, I think of Father Anthony, buried not long ago in this windswept cemetery that faces the rising sun. The hermitage is tucked on its south slope near a grove of trees. Sunset is a faint red line, the horizon smudged with rain. Anthony's observatory already has an abandoned air; I wonder if anyone will use it. The first time I came here he lent me his copy of *Burnham's Celestial Handbook* and I read of the Great Nebula in Orion that "it transports the imaginative observer back to the days of creation . . . and is undoubtedly one of the regions in space where star formation is presently underway."

Last summer I found Anthony slumped in his wheelchair under the crucifix in the east hallway. "Too much going on," he said, as young women in satin ballgowns passed by, patting their hair. A young monk hurried after them on his way to ring bells for the wedding Mass.

"A girl would come to the grocery," he said. "Etoile Mc-Kenna. I was fourteen. She had black hair, the fairest skin you ever saw. My brother said, 'Don'tcha get it? There's other stores in town. She's sweet on you. Don'tcha get it?' " and Anthony laughed, the stubble of his beard creasing like an old map.

Late last fall, I sat with him on a bench outside the monastery and watched dazed yellow jackets crawl on the bits of apple we put on the ground. When the stars began to come out, he named them all, his friends. He'd been a monk for more than fifty years and he said, "Heaven's gonna be great. Do you know the best thing I ever did? I made a clock that keeps star-time."

FRONTIER

To all earth's creatures God has given the broad earth,
the springs, the rivers and the forests, [giving] the air
to the birds, and the waters to those who live in
water, [giving] abundantly to all the basic needs of life,
not as a private possession, not restricted by law,
not divided by boundaries, but as common to all,
amply and in rich measure.
— GREGORY OF NAZIANZUS

LEMMON, SOUTH DAKOTA, IS HERE BECAUSE in 1908 the
United States government, responding to pressures that had
been building since the 1860s, opened up the last piece of
"Indian Territory" on the Standing Rock Reservation to homesteaders, and the Milwaukee Road pushed west with a railroad
line to accommodate them. In 1907 Lemmon was a tent city for
railroad workers, but the town soon had wooden sidewalks,
churches, a school, and businesses for farmers attracted by the
railroad's promotion of a mythical land of opportunity. Agron-
omists predicted that rain would follow the plow.

The ethnic make-up of the area still reflects the fact that the
Milwaukee Road advertised heavily in Scandinavia, while
about fifty miles to the north the Great Northern attracted
settlers from Germany as well as Germans who had farmed
since the time of Catherine the Great in south Russia. German

can still be heard on the streets of New Leipzig, North Dakota, where only a radical nonconformist would hang out laundry on any day but Monday. The Native American population is still concentrated to the east and south of Lemmon, around McLaughlin and Faith.

Frontier has all too often been romanticized in American culture by movies and novels glorifying the violent and often ugly code of the West. The fact that one people's frontier is usually another's homeland has been mostly overlooked. The names of the first inhabitants of western Dakota are lost to us. Descendants of the Mandans moved west from the Mississippi Valley early in the fourteenth century: they were followed in the early seventeenth century by the Hidatsa, who came from western Minnesota, and the Arikara, who came up the Missouri from Nebraska. These three tribes formed what the historian Elwyn B. Robinson has called "the distinctive culture of western Dakota, that of agricultural villages along the Missouri."

They were all but wiped out in the mid-eighteenth century by the nomadic Dakota (nicknamed "Sioux" by whites), who were pushed onto the Plains from Wisconsin and Minnesota by the more numerous Ojibway, who had obtained guns from French traders. More whites followed with U.S. Army posts. The late nineteenth century brought the Black Hills gold rush, and ranchers who seized vast tracts of native hunting lands for grazing, and who were later displaced by homesteaders. Now, as today's farmers and ranchers are being driven off the land and there's talk of using the Dakotas as a national garbage dump or a buffalo commons, I've come to think that one thing that distinguishes a frontier is the precarious nature of the human hold on it.

The severe climate of Dakota forces us to see that no one can control this land. The largeness of land and sky is humbling, putting humankind in proper perspective. A friend, Jim Lein, has described what it's like to walk here: "One night, I sensed not only the curvature of the earth but its size and gravitational pull. This feeling is no doubt what holds people to the prairie, what leads prairie people to feel claustrophobic in more cluttered environs, with their trees and mountains and tall buildings obscuring our view, our sense of planet."

This "sense of planet" allows Dakotans to feel as if they are in the middle of the world rather than, as others would have it, in the middle of nowhere. It also suggests to me the truth of what Native American writer Paula Gunn Allen said in a recent interview, that the longer Europeans remain in America, the more Indian they will become. "What makes an Indian an Indian," she explains, is a deep connection to the land, built over generations, "that imbues their psychology and eventually their spirituality and makes them one with the spirit of the land."

While this comment is vulnerable to a simplistic interpretation, and Dakotans grow weary of tourists claiming to be one with the land, let alone Indian at heart, after week-long camping trips in the Black Hills, Allen touches on a deep truth. The spirit of the land is not an abstraction in western Dakota, but a real presence. For people like the young white rancher I know, a third-generation Dakotan who says "the land lives," I wonder if what Allen suggests isn't already happening. I wonder if this process is what gave me the nerve to lay claim to my spiritual geography.

Not that I would claim to be Indian, or even to have a particularly deep understanding of Indian spirituality or way of life. I don't; and this is an important point to make in a confused era when many middle-class Americans, having rejected their own religious heritage, are seeking the sacred in Native American spirituality, often appropriating it in ways that add to the already bitter experience Indians have of being overwhelmed and consumed by white culture.

I suspect that when modern Americans ask "what is sacred?" they are really asking "what place is mine? what community do I belong to?" I think this explains in part the appeal of Native American religions, and also the appearance of guidebooks to monastic retreat houses. We are seeking the tribal, anything with strong communal values and traditions. But all too often we're trying to do it on our own, as individuals. That *is* the tradition of middle-class America; a belief in individual accomplishment so strong that it favors exploitation over stewardship, mobility over stability. That we pay a high price for applying upward mobility to the life of the spirit, denying roots, and turning a blind eye to that which might nurture us in our own heritage has been evident to at least one Native American writer. Linda Hogan speaks eloquently of her discovery

that many of (my) non-Indian students are desperately searching for spirits, for their own souls, that something in the contemporary world has left many Euro-Americans and Europeans without a source, has left them with a longing for something they believe existed in earlier times or in tribal people. What they want is their own life, their own love for the earth, but when they speak their own words about it, they don't believe them, so they look to Indians, forgetting that

enlightenment can't be found in a weekend workshop, forgetting that most Indian people are living the crisis of American life, the toxins of chemical waste, the pain of what is
repressed in white Americans. There is not such a thing as
becoming an instant shaman, an instant healer, an instantly
spiritualized person.

Traditional religions take for granted the truth of Hogan's
last statement, but Americans seek the quick fix for spiritual as
well as physical pain. That conversion is a lifelong process is
the last thing we want to hear. That it may reach back into
the generations before us, that the wisdom of what I might
term a cloud of witnesses or Linda Hogan calls watchers, to
describe visitors from the Indian spirit world, might still be
raging in our blood, having plenty to say to us, is even more
threatening.

Like Linda Hogan, I find a great spiritual hunger among
many people who are uncomfortable with talk of God, let alone
the idea of church. Many of them are rightfully rejecting the
distorted images of Christianity that they absorbed in childhood at the hands of too often ignorant catechism and Sunday
school instructors. It's a past most of us would like to forget.
But simply denying it won't work; and inventing Indian ancestors only clouds the real issue, which is fear.

Fear is not a bad place to start a spiritual journey. If you know
what makes you afraid, you can see more clearly that the way
out is through the fear. For me, this has meant acknowledging that the strong emotions dredged up by the few Christian worship services — usually weddings or funerals — I attended during the twenty-year period when I would have
described my religion as "nothing," were trying to tell me

something. It has meant coming to terms with my fundamentalist Methodist ancestors, no longer ignoring them but re-
specting their power.

Conversion means starting with who we are, not who we
wish we were. It means knowing where we come from. It
means taking to heart the words of Native American writer
Andy Smith, who writes in *Ms.*, "a true medicine woman
would . . . advise a white woman to look into her own culture
and find what is liberating in it." And this is what I hope I have
done, beginning with my move back to Dakota. My path of
conversion may have a few elements of Indianness, because of
the spirits of the land where I live, and because I understand
that my faith comes from my grandmothers. It was in moving
back to the Plains that I found my old ones, my flesh and blood
ancestors as well as the desert monks and mystics of the Christian church. Dakota is where it all comes together, and surely
that is one definition of the sacred.

It came as an unwelcome surprise that my old ones led me
back to church. It continues to surprise me that the church is
for me both a new and an old frontier. And it astonishes me as
much as it delights me that moving to the Dakota grasslands
led me to a religious frontier where the new growth is fed by
something very old, the 1,500-year tradition of Benedictine
monasticism. It grounds me; I use it as compost to "work
the earth of my heart," to borrow a phrase from a fourth-
century monk. I can long for change, for a "new earth," as
Gregory of Nyssa defines it, "a good heart, a heart like the
earth, which drinks up the rain that falls on it and yields a rich
harvest."

Conversion doesn't offer a form of knowledge that can be

bought and sold, quantified, or neatly packaged. It is best learned slowly and in community, the way a Native American child learns his or her traditional religion, the way an adult learns to be a Benedictine, not by book learning or weekend workshops but by being present at the ceremonies. Truly present, with a quiet heart that allows you to become a good listener, an observer of those — plants, animals, cloud formations, people, and words — who know and define the territory.

One of the earliest Christian monks, the fourth-century Anthony of the Desert, told a visiting philosopher who had apparently commented on his lack of reading material, "My book, O philosopher, is the nature of created things, and any time I wish to read the words of God, the book is before me." I know plenty of Dakotans, white and Native American alike, who feel the same way. In his *Life of Anthony*, Athanasius describes the mountain in the desert where the saint finally settled as a hermit, saying that "Anthony, as though inspired by God, fell in love with the place." Ecologist Susan Bratton has pointed out that the Greek verb used for "fell in love" in this sentence is a form of *agapao*, which implies a love that is divinely ordained.

The hermit stories of desert and Celtic monasticism are full of monks in love with a place, and the Christian mystical and monastic tradition often acts as a countercultural stream in a religion which has over-emphasized the spiritual. Bernard of Clairvaux, a monk in the tradition of Anthony, wrote in 1130 to a man who wanted to found a monastery, "Believe us who have experience, you will find much more laboring amongst woods than ever you will amongst books. Woods and stones will teach you more than any master."

Bernard's words remind me that it is the land of western Dakota that has taught me that communal worship is something I need; that it is an experience, not a philosophy or even theology. Whatever the pitch of my religious doubts, it is available to me for the asking. It seems a wonder to me that in our dull little town we can gather together to sing some great hymns, reflect on our lives, hear some astonishing scriptures (and maybe a boring sermon; you take your chances), offer some prayers and receive a blessing.

At its Latin root, the word religion is linked to the words ligature and ligament, words having both negative and positive connotations, offering both bondage and freedom of movement. For me, religion is the ligament that connects me to my grandmothers, who, representing so clearly the negative and positive aspects of the Christian tradition, made it impossible for me either to reject or accept the religion wholesale. They made it unlikely that I would settle for either the easy answers of fundamentalism or the overintellectualized banalities of a conventionally liberal faith. Instead, the more deeply I've reclaimed what was good in their faith, the more they have set me free to find my own way.

Step by step, as I made my way back to church, I began to find that many of the things modern people assume are irrelevant — the liturgical year, the liturgy of the hours, the Incarnation as an everyday reality — are in fact essential to my identity and my survival. I'm not denying the past, or trying to bring it back, but am seeking in my inheritance what theologian Letty Russell terms "a usable past." Perhaps I am also redefining frontier not as a place you exploit and abandon but as a place where you build on the past for the future. When we journey here, we discover it is no less old than new. T. S. Eliot wrote, "The end of all our exploring / Will be to arrive where we started / And know the place for the first time." Against all the odds, I rediscovered the religion I was born to, and found in it a home.

How I Came to Drink
My Grandmother's Piano

———◆———

I gave it to a church up the street. For over ten years I'd used it as a bookshelf and dust-collector and finally needed the space for more books. Now it makes music again, and that fact is for me a morsel of success in the face of my inertia, my sloth, my failures.

Failure is important in Dakota, but we don't like to talk about it. Failure surrounds us in boarded-up Main Streets and three generations of abandoned farmhouses scattered in the countryside.

I found my way to the Plains as a poet, someone who by training and experience had come to appreciate the small things of this world. Like the monk in contemplation, or the farmer who meditates to the sound and rhythm of his tractor and baler, I can sometimes see the seemingly insignificant detail for what it is.

I was snowed in at a mobile home in a town called Regent when Rita broke out the dandelion wine, reaching to a top shelf for glasses that were much too fancy for our thrown-together meal of hamburgers and fried potatoes. "A friend gave these to me," Rita said. "She said she never used them."

I began to hear that piano as Rita poured the wine. The dandelions spun around, glad to be yellow again, glad to be free of the dark.

STATUS
Or, Should Farmers Read Plato?

IT'S HARD TO TALK about western Dakota without mentioning Jell-O. A salad, in local parlance, is a dish made with Jell-O: lime Jell-O with Cool-Whip and sliced bananas; cherry Jell-O with fruit cocktail and miniature marshmallows; lemon Jell-O with grated carrots, celery, sliced green olives, and walnuts for a fancy touch.

To understand the real meaning of Jell-O in Dakota, one has to think in terms of status. Status and electricity. It wasn't until the advent of electric refrigeration that Jell-O became a staple of the potluck supper or the women's club luncheon, and that meant town women could serve Jell-O long before country women. Jell-O remained elusive for the most remote rural women until well into the 1950s. Statistics can give some perspective on this. In 1925, when 53.2 percent of American homes had electricity, the figure for eastern North Dakota was 38.8 percent and for western North Dakota, 2.9 percent.

The deprivations of Dakota life can deliver a generational jolt: a man in his early forties reminisces about the time his mother rode twenty-four miles roundtrip on horseback after a blizzard to the snow-bound country school to get textbooks for him and his three brothers and sisters; people in their fifties speak of being born and raised in sod houses; a woman in her nineties recalls riding across South Dakota in a covered wagon. These are anachronistic memories, and even today many Dakotans live in a world remote from mainstream America. One year the Prairie Winds high school writers workshop was unable to use its usual rugged Black Hills lodge, and we had to scramble at the last moment for a place, finally settling on the Holiday Inn in Spearfish, on the northwest edge of the Hills. I assumed we'd have trouble keeping the teenagers from spending too much time at the video games or in the pool. We underestimated them: despite the distractions, they worked hard on their writing. We did have trouble over the plumbing, though. We found that some of the Native American students live in homes without indoor plumbing — their school opens early in the morning so they can bathe — and many of the white students had never before stayed in a motel. One girl from an isolated ranch in south-central South Dakota, used to a tin shower stall in a half-finished basement, was so intimidated by the fancy bathroom fixtures that she began to cry. Several of the writers conducted impromptu orientation sessions on how the bathrooms worked.

What does status mean in a world so at odds with American society? By that I mean not simply the America of middle-class whites but that of our richly diverse cities where people of many races live and many languages are spoken. The divisions created by status stand out so starkly in Dakota if only because its population is so sparse. In a way, we are a microcosm of the tribalism that is reasserting itself in the world. Even in homogenous Dakota we're finding out that we don't speak the same language after all. Hard times pit our small cities against our larger ones, and small cities grow at the expense of the attrition in small towns. In the genre of North Dakota jokes my favorite is: What's the motto of the North Dakota Workers' Union? Every man for himself.

When people in Lemmon speak of the economic depression of the 1920s and 1930s they tend to say things like, "We never felt poor because everyone was in the same boat; we were all poor together." While I suspect that this is not really how it was, I know that there is some truth to it. My grandfather, a doctor, had more money than most. But during the worst of the depression my grandmother often wouldn't know what supper was to be until her husband came home from the office with a chicken or hunk of mutton that a farmer had given him in payment of a bill. My mother recalls that in those days her mother made the family underwear from flour sacks.

The long memories of Dakota people — I once inadvertently grieved a man in Lemmon who had been sweet on my mother in high school by wearing a ring he'd given her nearly fifty years before — still carry many wounds from the Depression era, wounds caused by lack of status. Small-town society often reminds me of the old joke about academic politics — they're so vicious because there's so little at stake. A country woman who had helped my grandmother clean house for many years told me that she had been one of her few employers who would speak to her on Main Street.

In rural areas such as mine, many external signs of division by status lessened after World War II and the advent of the automobile. But one farmer told me she regrets the way the car destroyed the living room dances that used to be held on Saturday nights in the country, three generations or more gathering to dance to 78s or music on the radio. High school students who until the mid-1970s would rent rooms in Lemmon through the winter now drive their cars into town every day, except in exceptionally bad weather, when they stay with relatives or friends rather than risk the country roads.

The automobile blurred distinctions between town and country residents. By the 1970s, when teenagers began forming cliques of ropers (cowboy hats, rodeo clubs, pickup trucks, country and western music, beer) and dopers (long hair, black T-shirts, vans, marijuana, heavy metal, beer) status was no longer determined by where you lived. Some ropers lived in town, and many dopers were farm kids. The automobile also put an end to the second-class status of rural students in Lemmon and towns like it, enabling farm kids to participate in extracurricular activities instead of taking buses home right after school to do chores.

For years teachers assumed that rural kids wouldn't need reading, as a man in his forties recalls overhearing a teacher say about him. He's bright and curious and would like to read more than he does. He likes Edgar Allan Poe. But reading is a chore for him rather than a pleasure, and he knows he's lost a world. He'd like to read Plato, he says, but as a farmer struggling to hold onto his land and raise three boys on his own, he doesn't feel up to the task.

Dakota can be terrifying enough without the loss of one's cultural context. I know as well as anyone that a lot of book learning doesn't make a person wise (sometimes it simply legitimizes stupidity), but I can't help but connect the fact that so many Dakotans have been denied access to their culture with the fact that they don't trust that their own stories are worth much. But I speak of this at the risk of stirring up buried rage. Once, when I was being interviewed for a newspaper article, I mentioned that young farmer and was misquoted as saying that farmers would be happier if they read Plato. A woman wrote an angry letter to the editor, saying it made about as much sense as saying that poets would be happier if they could be pig farmers.

I've pondered this for years. Plato never made me particularly happy, but I'm glad to have had the chance to read him, and Dante, and Shakespeare, and the Brontës — eloquent human voices speaking through the centuries. I can't imagine life without them; I imagine I would feel like one of my monk friends when he has to be away from the monastery and its liturgy for any length of time. He says the world goes flat. I know that classics are attractive to people here when they stumble onto them. Once, in the public library, a waitress tired of romance novels asked me for something romantic, but with more to it. I offered her *Anna Karenina* and *Jane Eyre*, and she soon had all the other waitresses reading them. The books circulated for months.

I know that Mao tried to make pig farmers out of poets and that it didn't work too well for the poets; I don't know how the pigs fared. Where I live, there is no context for talking about either Plato or Mao. I know that Thomas Jefferson, who first read Plato's *Republic* in Greek at the age of seventy-one and found it overrated, believed that the independent farmer was a foundation stone of American democracy. But, knowing that the words for liberty and library come from the same Latin root, he also believed that the farmer had to be well read for democracy to work.

I wonder how viable Jefferson's vision of democracy is anymore, now that the human connection with the written word is largely lost. I wonder if in losing their sense of human accomplishment, of what is *possible* — the history of the space program is taught beginning in elementary school, airplanes fly overhead every day, and a television signal comes from a station over a hundred miles away, but a math teacher tells students that spherical trigonometry has no practical application — the young people of my town aren't becoming more like the disenfranchised youth of an urban ghetto, for whom education is also made to seem irrelevant. I wonder if I'm witnessing the creation of a new underclass: not only farmers on food stamps and young couples whose education prepares them for unskilled, low-paying work, but also those who own small businesses, and more successful farmers and ranchers whose lack of knowledge about the world makes it more and more difficult for them to compete in a global marketplace, to have any status at all.

"Who are those guys on the quarter, nickel, and dime?" asks a small group of young people, all graduates of high schools in the region. On being told, Washington, Jefferson, and Franklin Roosevelt, they seem to recognize only the name of Washington. "Which one of those countries is Communist, anyway," asks a high school junior, an honor-roll student, "China or Japan?"

Weather Report: July 3

◆

Rains came late in June and haying was delayed. But today it was 65 degrees by six A.M. and that means a hot day, 100 degrees or more; it means haying can't wait.

It's one of the miracles of nature that this empty-looking land can be of such great use, that cattle can convert its grasses to milk and meat.

I know that the brome and wheatgrass will lose its value as feed if it isn't hayed soon, but ever since I moved to Dakota I've felt a kind of grief at haying time. I hate to see the high grass fall.

Alfalfa and clover still stand tall by the road, smelling sweet and clean, like a milkfed infant's breath. In a few days these vigorous plants will be coffin-size heaps in the ditch.

RAIN

Above all, it is a land in serious need of rain.
— WILLIAM C. SHERMAN, *Plains Folk*

UNTIL I MOVED to western South Dakota, I did not know about rain, that it could come too hard, too soft, too hot, too cold, too early, too late. That there could be too little at the right time, too much at the wrong time, and vice versa.

I did not know that a light rain coming at the end of a hot afternoon, with the temperature at 100 degrees or more, can literally burn wheat, steaming it on the stalk so it's not worth harvesting.

I had not seen a long, slow rain come at harvest, making grain lying in the swath begin to sprout again, ruining it as a cash crop.

Until I had seen a few violent hailstorms and replaced the shingles on our roof twice in five years, I had forgotten why my grandmother had screens made of chicken wire for all the windows on the west side of her house.

I had not seen the whimsy of wind, rain, and hail; a path in a wheatfield as if a drunken giant had stumbled through, leaving footprints here and there. I had not seen hail fall from a clear blue sky. I had not tasted horizontal rain, flung by powerful winds.

I had not realized that a long soaking rain in spring or fall, a straight-down-falling rain, a gentle, splashing rain is more than a blessing. It's a miracle.

An old farmer once asked my husband and me how long we'd been in the country. "Five years," we answered. "Well, then," he said, "you've seen rain."

SEA CHANGE

Calenture: a disease incident to sailors within the tropics,
characterized by delirium in which the patient, it is said,
fancies the sea to be green fields and desires to leap into it.
— *Oxford English Dictionary*

The atmosphere of the sea persists in Perkins County.
— DAVID J. HOLDEN, *Dakota Visions*

My MOVE FROM NEW YORK CITY to western South Dakota
changed my sense of time and space so radically I might as well
have gone to sea. In journeying on the inland ocean of the
Plains, the great void at the heart of North America, I've discovered that time and distance, those inconveniences that modern
life with its increasingly sophisticated computer technologies
seeks to erase, have a reality and a terrifying beauty all their
own.

Like all who choose life in the slow lane — sailors, monks,
farmers — I partake of a contemplative reality. Living close to
such an expanse of land I find I have little incentive to move
fast, little need of instant information. I have learned to trust
the processes that take time, to value change that is not sudden
or ill-considered but grows out of the ground of experience.
Such change is properly defined as conversion, a word that at
its root connotes not a change of essence but of perspective, as

turning round; turning back to or returning; turning one's attention to.

Both monasteries and the rural communities on the Plains are places where nothing much happens. Paradoxically, they are also places where being open to conversion is most necessary if community is to survive. The inner impulse toward conversion, a change of heart, may be muted in a city, where outward change is fast, noisy, ever-present. But in the small town, in the quiet arena, a refusal to grow (which is one way Gregory of Nyssa defined sin) makes any constructive change impossible. Both monasteries and small towns lose their ability to be truly hospitable to the stranger when people use them as a place to hide out, a place to escape from the demands of life.

Because of the monotony of the monastic life, the bad thought of boredom (or acedia, the noonday demon) has traditionally been thought to apply particularly to monks, but I think most people have endured a day or two along the lines of this fourth-century description by the monk Evagrius:

> It makes it seem that the sun barely moves, if at all, and the day is fifty hours long. Then it constrains the monk to look constantly out the window, to walk outside the cell to gaze carefully at the sun and determine how far it stands from the dinner hour, to look now this way and that to see if perhaps one of the brethren appears from his cell.

Anyone living in isolated or deprived circumstances, whether in a monastery or a quiet little town on the Great Plains, is susceptible to the noonday demon. It may appear as an innocuous question; "Isn't the mail here yet?" But, as monks have always known, such restlessness can lead to profound despair that makes a person despise his or her neighbors, work, and even life itself. Perhaps the noonday demon helps explain the high rate of alcoholism found in underpopulated steppes, whether in Siberia or the American West.

Ever since moving to western Dakota, I've wondered if the version of the demon we experience here isn't a kind of calenture, a prairie version of the sea fever that afflicted sailors several centuries ago. The vast stretch of undulating land before us can make us forget ourselves, make us do foolish things.

I almost think that to be a good citizen of the Plains one must choose the life consciously, as one chooses the monastery. One must make an informed rejection of any other way of life and also undergo a period of formation. Some of the ranch families I know in Dakota are raising their children in the way Benedict asks monasteries to treat would-be monks, warning, "Do not grant newcomers to the monastic life an easy entry."

These parents do not encourage their children to take up the hard and economically uncertain life of farming and ranching. Instead, they provide them with the opportunity to see what is available in other careers, in other places. And most of the young people move on. But, as one couple recently told me of their daughter, "She's traveled, she's seen the outside world. And it's not that she's afraid of it or couldn't live there, she's decided she doesn't need it. She wants to come back here."

They're hoping she will find a teaching job in the area, not a great prospect in the current economic environment, when many Dakota schools are consolidating or closing. But what interests me about her parents' remark is how like monastic formation directors they sound. They, too, want people who have lived a little, who have seen the world, and, in the words of one monk, "know exactly what it is they're giving up." He added, "The hard part is that this has to become all they need. The monastery has to become their home."

Making the Plains a home means accepting its limitations and not, as so many townspeople do even in drought years, watering a lawn to country club perfection. Making this all we need means accepting that we are living in the arid plains of western South Dakota, not in Connecticut (which has the rainfall to sustain such greenery) or Palm Springs (which doesn't but has the money to pretend otherwise). Once the water runs out, the money won't be worth much.

I wonder if the calentures don't explain why, from the first days of white settlement, Dakotans of the West River have tried to recreate the land before them in the image of the rain-blessed places they knew, the rich farmland back East in New York or Virginia, or the old country farmland of Sweden, or Scotland. Encouraged by the railroads and the government to pretend that the land could support families on homestead allotments of 160 acres, they believed the rural economy could maintain small towns nine or ten miles apart, the distance a steam locomotive could go before needing more water. But, in trying to make this place like the places they had known, they would not allow it to be itself.

Eastern North and South Dakota have enough rainfall and population density to hang on at the western fringes of the Midwest, having more in common with Minnesota and Iowa than with Montana. But in western Dakota, the harsh climate and the vast expanse of the land have forced people, through a painful process of attrition, to adjust to this country on its own terms and live accordingly: ranches of several thousand acres, towns that serve as economic centers forty or sixty miles apart.

Taking the slow boat to Dakota, driving in from the East, the reality of the land asserts itself and you begin to understand how the dreams of early settlers were worn away.

Heading west out of Minneapolis on Highway 12, you pass through 150 miles of rich Minnesota farmland, through towns that look like New England villages with tall trees well over a hundred years old. These are sizeable towns by Dakota standards: Litchfield (pop. 5,900), Willmar (15,900), Benson (3,600). South Dakota is visible, a high ridge on the horizon, long before the crossing a few miles past Ortonville (pop. 2,550, elev. 1,094).

Your first town in South Dakota is Big Stone City (pop. 630, elev. 977) at the southern edge of Big Stone Lake, named for huge granite outcroppings in the area. Here you begin your climb from the broad Minnesota River Valley to what French trappers termed the "Coteau des Prairies" or prairie hills of eastern South Dakota. This is the beginning of the drift prairie of eastern North and South Dakota, named for the glacial deposits, or drift, that make up its topsoil. The road narrows, twisting around small hills and shallow coulees. You pass by several small, spring-fed lakes formed by glaciers and several good-size towns: Milbank (pop. 3,800), Webster (2,000), Groton (1,100).

After Groton you cross the James River Valley, its soil rich with glacial loam deposits. By the time you reach the city of Aberdeen, South Dakota (pop. 25,000, elev. 1,304), one hundred miles from the Minnesota border, you are in open farm country with more of a gentle roll to it than eastern Kansas, but basically flat and treeless except for shelterbelts around farmhouses and trees planted and carefully tended in the towns.

Driving west from Aberdeen you find that the towns are fewer and smaller, with more distance between them: Ipswich (pop. 965), Roscoe (362), Bowdle (590), Selby (707). One hundred miles west of Aberdeen you come to Mobridge (pop. 3,768, elev. 1,676), on the banks of the Missouri River.

What John Steinbeck said in *Travels with Charley* about the Missouri River crossing 120 miles to the north is true of the Mobridge crossing as well. He wrote: "Here's the boundary between east and west. On the Bismarck side it is eastern landscape, eastern grass, with the look and smell of eastern America. Across the Missouri on the Mandan side it is pure west with brown grass and water scorings and small outcrops. The two sides of the river might well be a thousand miles apart."

The boundary is an ancient one. The deep gorge of the Missouri marks the western edge of the Wisconsin ice sheet that once covered most of north central America. Passing through Mobridge and crossing the river you take a steep climb through rugged hills onto the high plateau that extends west all the way to the Rockies. Lewis and Clark marked this border by noting that the tallgrass to the east (bluestem, switch grass, Indian grass) grew six to eight feet high, while the shortgrass in the west (needle-and-thread, western wheat grass, blue grama grass, and upland sedges) topped at about four feet. You have left the glacial drift prairie for a land whose soil is the residue of prehistoric seas that have come and gone, weathered shale and limestone that is far less fertile than the land to the east but good for grazing sheep and cattle. Here you set your watch to Mountain time.

Here, also, you may have to combat disorientation and an overwhelming sense of loneliness. Plunged into the pale expanse of shortgrass country, you either get your sea legs or want to bail out. As the road twists and turns through open but hilly country, climbing 325 feet in twenty-two miles to the town of McLaughlin (pop. 780), you begin to realize you have left civilization behind. You are on the high plains, where there are almost no trees, let alone other people. You find that the towns reassuringly listed every ten miles or so on your map (Walker, McIntosh, Watauga, Morristown, Keldron, Thunder Hawk) offer very little in the way of services. All but McIntosh (pop. 300) have populations well under a hundred. You climb imperceptibly through rolling hayfields and pasture land punctuated by wheat or sunflower fields for another eighty miles or so before you reach another town of any size — Lemmon (pop. 1,616, elev. 2,577).

You should have filled your gas tank in Aberdeen, especially if you're planning to travel after dark. For many years there was no gasoline available at night (except in the summer) between Aberdeen and Miles City, Montana, a distance of nearly four hundred miles. Currently there are two 24-hour stations in towns nearly 200 miles apart. On the last stretch, the 78 miles from Baker, Montana, to Miles City, there are no towns at all, just a spectacularly desolate moonscape of sagebrush. Farmers will usually give or sell a little gas to stranded travelers, and small-town police forces often have keys to the local service stations so they can sell you enough to get you on your way. But the message is clear: you're in the West now. Pay attention to your gas gauge. Pay attention, period.

But it's hard to pay attention when there is so much nothing to take in, so much open land that evokes in many people a panicked desire to get through it as quickly as possible. A writer whose name I have forgotten once remarked, "Driving through eastern Montana is like waiting for Godot." I know this only because a Lemmon Public Library patron brought me the quote, wanting to know who or what Godot was. It struck me that the writer may as well have been talking about the landscape of Dakota from Mobridge or Mandan west. And it seemed appropriate that the good citizen of the region wanted to know if her homeland was being praised or put down. Had he lived here, I wonder if Beckett would have found it necessary to write the play.

But people do live here, and many of them will tell you in all honesty that they wouldn't live anyplace else. Monks often say the same thing about their monasteries, and get the same looks of incomprehension. People who can't imagine not having more stimulation in their lives will ask, "How can you do it?" or, "Why do it?" If those questions are answerable for either a monk or a Plains resident, they can't be answered in a few quick words but in the slow example of a lifetime. The questioner must take the process of endless waiting into account, as well as the pull of the sea change, of conversion.

Often, when I'm sitting in a monastery choir stall, I wonder how I got there. I could trace it back, as I can trace the route from back East to western South Dakota. But I'm having too much fun. The words of Psalms, spoken aloud and left to resonate in the air around me, push me into new time and space. I think of it as the quantum effect: here time flows back and forth, in and out of both past and future, and I, too, am changed.

Being continually open to change, to conversion, is a Benedictine ideal: in fact, it's a vow unique to those who follow Benedict's *Rule*. This might seem like a paradox, as monks, like farmers, stay in one place and have a daily routine that can seem monotonous even to them. But the words spark like a welder's flame; they keep flowing, like a current carrying me farther than I had intended to go. At noon prayer we hear the scripture about "sharing the lot of the saints in light," and in the afternoon I read in a book about quantum physics that some scientists believe that one day everything will exist in the form of light. At vespers the text is from I John: "Beloved, we are God's children now; what we will be has not yet been revealed."

The sun is setting and a nearly full, fat-faced moon is rising above the prairie. We have time on our hands here, in our hearts, and it makes us strange. I barely passed elementary algebra, but somehow the vast space before me makes perfectly comprehensible the words of a mathematician I encountered today: it is easy to "demonstrate that there are no more minutes in all of eternity than there are in say, one minute."

The vespers hymn reads: "May God ever dress our days / in peace and starlight order," and I think of old Father Stanley, who said not long before he died: "I wish to see the Alpha and the Omega." He'd been a monk for over fifty years, a Dakotan for more than eighty. It's a dangerous place, this vast ocean of prairie. Something happens to us here.

God Is in the Details: Shortgrass

———————◆———————

He said: "You want to hay your brome and crested wheatgrass. They're the taller, more lush grasses, not native, and they'll lose their nutritive value quickly. Any moisture and they'll frost-kill. But the native shortgrass — that's your grama and buffalo grass, sedges and switch grass — makes for good winter pasture. You let it stand, and it cures on the stem."

SEEING

The midwestern landscape is abstract, and our response to
the geology of the region might be similar to our response
to the contemporary walls of paint in museums.
We are forced to live in our eye.
— MICHAEL MARTONE

Abba Bessarion, at the point of death, said, "The monk
ought to be like the Cherubim and the Seraphim: all eye."
— *The Desert Christian*

ONCE, WHEN I WAS DESCRIBING to a friend from Syra-
cuse, New York, a place on the plains that I love, a ridge above
a glacial moraine with a view of almost fifty miles, she asked,
"But what is there to see?"

The answer, of course, is nothing. Land, sky, and the ever-
changing light. Except for a few signs of human presence —
power and telephone lines, an occasional farm building, the
glint of a paved road in the distance — it's like looking at the
ocean.

The landscape of western Dakota is not as abstract as the flats
of Kansas, but it presents a similar challenge to the eye that
appreciates the vertical definition of mountains or skyscrapers;
that defines beauty in terms of the spectacular or the busy:
hills, trees, buildings, highways, people. We seem empty by
comparison.

Here, the eye learns to appreciate slight variations, the possibilities inherent in emptiness. It sees that the emptiness is full of small things, like grasshoppers in their samurai armor clicking and jumping as you pass. This empty land is full of grasses: sedges, switch grass, needlegrass, wheatgrass. Brome can grow waist-high by early summer. Fields of wheat, rye, oats, barley, flax, alfalfa. Acres of sunflowers brighten the land in summer, their heads alert, expectant. By fall they droop like sad children, waiting patiently for the first frost and harvest.

In spring it is a joy to discover, amid snow and mud and pale, withered grass, the delicate lavender of pasqueflower blooming on a ridge with a southern exposure. There is variety in the emptiness; the most prosaic pasture might contain hundreds of different wildflowers along with sage, yucca, and prairie cactus. Coulees harbor chokecherry, buffalo berry, and gooseberry bushes in their gentle folds, along with groves of silvery cottonwoods and Russian olive. Lone junipers often grow on exposed hillsides.

This seemingly empty land is busy with inhabitants. Low to the ground are bullsnakes, rattlers, mice, gophers, moles, grouse, prairie chickens, and pheasant. Prairie dogs are more noticeable, as they denude the landscape with their villages. Badgers and skunk lumber busily through the grass. Jackrabbits, weasels, and foxes are quicker, but the great runners of the Plains are the coyote, antelope, and deer. Meadowlarks, killdeer, blackbirds, lark buntings, crows, and seagulls dart above the fields, and a large variety of hawks, eagles, and vultures glide above it all, hunting for prey.

Along with the largeness of the visible — too much horizon, too much sky — this land's essential indifference to the human can be unnerving. We had a visitor, a friend from back East who flew into Bismarck and started a two-week visit by photographing the highway on the way to Lemmon; "Look how far you can see!" he kept exclaiming, trying to capture the whole of it in his camera lens. He seemed relieved to find a few trees in town and in our yard, and did not relish going back out into open country.

One night he called a woman friend from a phone booth on Main Street and asked her to marry him. After less than a week, he decided to cut his visit short and get off the Plains. He and his fiancée broke off the engagement, mutually and amicably, not long after he got home to Boston. The proposal had been a symptom of "Plains fever."

A person is forced inward by the spareness of what is outward and visible in all this land and sky. The beauty of the Plains is like that of an icon; it does not give an inch to sentiment or romance. The flow of the land, with its odd twists and buttes, is like the flow of Gregorian chant that rises and falls beyond melody, beyond reason or human expectation, but perfectly.

Maybe seeing the Plains is like seeing an icon: what seems stern and almost empty is merely open, a door into some simple and holy state.

Not long ago, at a difficult time in my life, when my husband was recovering from surgery, I attended a drum ceremony with a Native American friend. Men and boys gathered around the sacred drum and sang a song to bless it. Their singing was high-pitched, repetitive, solemn, and loud. As they approached the song's end, drumming louder and louder, I realized that the music was also restorative; my two-day headache was gone, my troubles no longer seemed so burdensome.

I wondered how this loud, shrill, holy music, the indigenous song of those who have truly seen the Plains, could be so restful, while the Gregorian chant that I am just learning to sing can be so quiet, and yet as stirring as any drum. Put it down to ecstasy.

Weather Report: August 9

◆

Some 250,000 motorcyclists converge on Sturgis in the Black Hills, boosting South Dakota's population by more than a third. Some two hundred Benedictine men and women gather in the opposite corner of the state, at a convent on the bluffs of the Missouri River.

It's hard to say which gathering is the more important; both are marked by partying and all manner of prayer.

I cast my lot with the monks and nuns. It matters to know where on earth we are. Yankton. The haze of late summer, complete with gnats. There is the Zen of it: "When you come to a place where you have to go left or right," says Sister Ruth, "go straight ahead."

GETTING TO HOPE

To GET TO HOPE, turn south off U.S. Highway 12 at Keldron, South Dakota. It's easy to miss, as the town is not much more than a gas station and general store with a well-kept house behind it, and a sign announcing that Cammy Varland of Keldron was Miss Teen South Dakota of 1987.

Turn onto the gravel section-line road and look for a wooden map on your right. Built by the Busy Beavers 4-H Club, it has the mysterious yet utilitarian air of the seashell, twine, and bamboo maps that South Sea islanders once made for navigational purposes. The Keldron map consists of wooden slats painted with names and numerical inscriptions. Peterson 8 s 4 E 1 N indicates that you would drive eight miles south, four miles east, and one mile north to find the Peterson ranch.

The small metal sign for Hope (13 s) may or may not be up. The wind pulls it down and it can be a while before someone notices and reattaches it. But you don't need directions; just follow the road south and turn when it turns 90 degrees west, then another 90 degrees south, and then it's just another mile or so.

Ten and a half miles along the road, at the crest of the second hill, you'll be able to see where you're going, a tiny ark in a sea of land that unfolds before you for nearly fifty miles. At night you can see the lights of Isabel, South Dakota, some forty-five

miles south, and Bison, about the same distance to the southwest.

The breaks of the Grand River are visible, land crumpled like
brown paper. The river itself lies at the base of the steep cliffs it
has carved into the prairie, sandstone glinting in the morning
sun. *Paha Sunkawakan Sapa*, or Black Horse Butte, is a brooding
presence on the horizon south of the river.

You will pass a few modest homes and farm buildings along
the way, some in use, others in disrepair. The most recently
abandoned, a classic two-story farmhouse, has boarded-up
windows and an extensive but weed-choked corral. A house
abandoned years ago is open to the elements, all its windows
and most of its shingles gone. A large shelterbelt, planted in
the 1930s, is now a thicket of dead trees. Once the trees are
gone the house will lean with the wind until it collapses; but
that will be a while.

Like the others who have business in Hope, I know who left;
I know why. Every time I pass the abandoned houses I am
reminded of them. "Hope Presbyterian Church is located by
itself on the South Dakota prairie," is what the church history
says. But that doesn't begin to tell it. Hope Church, which
fifteen years ago had a membership of 46, is down to 25 today,
scattered on ranches for thirty miles around. The loss is due to
older farmers retiring and moving to town, and younger farmers leaving the area.

Hope Church is an unassuming frame building that stands
in a pasture at the edge of a coulee where ash trees and berry
bushes flourish; chokecherry, snowberry, buffalo berry. The
place doesn't look like much, even when most of the membership has arrived on Sunday morning, yet it's one of the most

successful churches I know. Along with Center School, the one-room schoolhouse that currently serves nine children from Grand Valley, Riverside, and Rolling Green townships in southwest Corson County, Hope Church gives the people who live around it a sense of identity.

"It doesn't matter what religion they are," says one longtime member. "The Lutherans and Catholics tell us that Hope is important to them, too, and becoming more so. We're *the church* in the neighborhood." A former pastor said of Hope Church, "It seemed that whatever was going on, a farm sale or a funeral or wedding, Hope was a part of what happened in that community." A measure of this may be seen at the annual Vacation Bible School for children, which is attended by both Lutheran and Catholic children.

The current church was built by its members in 1961 on the cement foundation of an old barn. But its roots go back to 1916, when people gathered for Sunday worship in the dance halls of the small settlements at White Deer and Glad Valley. "Church wasn't awfully regular in the horse and buggy days," says an older member of Hope, the son of one of the founders. "The ministers at McIntosh or Thunder Hawk were circuit riders then, and it could take them half a day to get down to us." Neither congregation ever had a church building. Until they merged in 1950, one congregation met in a one-room school, and the other in a hall that served as a community center where baby showers, funeral luncheons, wedding dances, and anniversary celebrations are also held.

Hope is well cared for. Both the outhouse and the sanctuary are freshly painted. Two small, attractive stained glass windows depicting a cross in the center of a sunburst and a dove with an olive branch flying over a landscape that resembles the fields around Hope Church were recently added to the south wall behind the pulpit, placed on either side of a handmade cross of varnished wood. The elegantly curved oak pews with carved endpieces are hand-me-downs from a church in Minnesota. A member of Hope drove his grain truck more than three hundred miles to get them.

Hope has a noble and well-used upright piano whose sound reminds me of the honky-tonk pianos in Western movies. But when Carolyn plays her quiet-down music at the beginning of a service, "Shall We Gather at the River" or "Holy, Holy, Holy," she's as effective as a Russian Orthodox deacon striding sternly through a church with censer and bells. We know it's time now to listen, that we will soon take our journey into word and song, and maybe change a little along the way. By the time we're into our first hymn, we know where we are. To paraphrase Isaiah 62, it's a place no longer desolate but delightful.

There is no indoor plumbing at Hope, but the congregation celebrates with food and drink at every opportunity. Once, when I arrived on Sunday, I noticed several popcorn poppers in a back pew. That was for after church, to help everyone get through the annual congregational meeting. Once, Hope gave me a party with homemade cake, coffee and iced tea, and Kool-Aid in big coolers that the men carried into the basement.

In the manner of the other tiny country churches I know (United Tribes in Bismarck and Saint Philip's in Maili, Hawaii) Hope is such a hospitable place that I suspect that no matter who you are or where you come from, you will be made to feel at home. But don't get so comfortable that you underestimate the people around you; don't entertain for a moment the notion that these farmers and ranchers are quaint country folk. Most of them have college degrees, though the figure is down slightly from 85 percent in the mid-1980s, a statistic that startled the pastor, who had last worked in Scranton, Pennsylvania, where 3 percent of her congregation was college educated.

Hope's people read, and they think about what is going on in the world. If you want to know anything about agriculture on a global scale — the cattle market in Argentina or prospects for the wheat crop in Australia — this is the place to ask. As one pastor recently put it, "the thing that makes Hope so vibrant is that the congregation is so alive to the world."

Hope's members take seriously their responsibility as members of the world's diverse and largely poor human race. A few years ago, reasoning that people who raise food (and often have a hard time getting a price for it that covers their expenses) should know more about why so many in the world can't afford to feed themselves, they conducted a study of the politics of hunger. To conclude the study they invited an expert on the subject to come from Chicago to address churchpeople in the area. They also studied the ethical issues of raising animals for food. As ranchers who know the life history and temperament of every cow in their herds, they were dismayed to discover the inroads factory farming had made in American agriculture.

In recent hard times, while Hope's membership declined by nearly half, the amount the church donates for mission has increased every year. It now ranks near the top in per capita giving among Presbyterian churches in the state of South Dakota.

One former pastor said, "It can be astonishing how tiny Hope Church makes you feel so strongly that you're part of a global entity." This is a long tradition at Hope. A rancher whose three daughters spent several years in ecumenical church work in Sydney, Paris, Rome, and Brussels says: "Our girls always knew that the world was bigger than just us. They had cousins who were missionaries in China in the 1950s and 1960s. In those days missionaries got every seventh year off, and they'd stay with us on the ranch. Our children grew up hearing stories about other places."

For this and other reasons pastors find the Hope congregation stimulating to work with. One told me if he could sum them up in one word it would be "appreciative." Another said: "Hope was where I realized how much the members of a rural church actually work as well as worship together. They live supporting each other. We'd spoken of such things at seminary, as an ideal, but this was the first time in twenty years of ministry I'd actually seen it done. It made me realize how vital a small country church can be."

Perhaps it's not surprising that so tiny a rural congregation is not often well served by the larger church of which it is a part. For all their pious talk of "small is beautiful," church bureaucrats, like bureaucrats everywhere, concentrate their attention on places with better demographics; bigger numbers, more power and money. The power of Hope Church and country churches like it is subtle and not easily quantifiable. It's a power derived from smallness and lack of power, a concept the apostle Paul would appreciate, even if modern church bureaucrats lose sight of it.

In the manner of country people everywhere (and poets also for that matter) the people at Hope tend to be conservators of language. Once, when I found myself staggering through a benediction provided by the denomination that, among other things, invited us to "authenticate the past," I stopped and said, "I'm sorry, but that's ridiculous English." Laughter became our benediction that morning.

Like most small churches in the western Dakotas, Hope must be yoked to another, larger church in order to afford a full-time pastor. When Hope's sister church in Lemmon, thirty miles away, received memorial money to purchase a new Presbyterian hymnal that includes many contemporary hymns and more inclusive language, Hope decided to stay with their 1955 model. Not because its members aren't progressive. It's a relatively youthful congregation, in fact, with nary a fundamentalist bone among them. But the old hymnal works well for them, and many of their standards are not included in the new book: "I Need Thee Every Hour" and "I Love to Tell the Story" (which, not surprisingly, has been a favorite of mine since childhood), and "Nearer, My God, to Thee." That last hymn was a revelation to me when I first came back to church. Like many people, I couldn't think of it without picturing the band on the Titanic in *A Night to Remember*. I was pleased to discover that the hymn is an evocative retelling of the story of Jacob's dream.

As one pastor of Hope, a graduate of Princeton seminary, said to me, "Church intellectuals always want to root out the pietistic hymns, but in a rural area like this those hymns of intimacy are necessary for the spiritual welfare of people who are living at such a distance from each other." He added, "City people want hymns that reassure them that God is at work in the world, but people in the western Dakotas take that for granted."

The conflict between urban and rural theologies is an old one in the Christian church. Back in fourth-century Egypt, the Bishop of Alexandria, at the urging of intellectuals smitten with Greek philosophy, announced as church doctrine that when you pray you must not have any picture of God in your mind.

One old monk is reported to have wept, saying, "They have taken away my God, and I have none I can hold now, and know not whom to adore or to address myself." Some monks took to their boats and traveled the Nile to Alexandria, where they rioted in front of the bishop's palace until he recanted. Hope's people have been more quiet about letting the greater Church go its way.

I find it ironic that the new inclusiveness of the official church tends to exclude people as rural as those of Hope. But I may have been spoiled by the company I keep on the prairie, the Benedictine monks and country people, some well educated, some not, who know from their experience that prayer is important, that worship serves a purpose, that God is part of everyday life, and that singing "Nearer My God, to Thee" may be good for a person. It's a rural hymn: it's the rare city person who can imagine sleeping out in the open, a stone for a pillow and a heaven of stars above.

Maybe we're all anachronisms in Dakota, a bunch of hicks, and the fact that the images in many old hymns, images of seed and wheat, planting and reaping, images as old as the human race and as new as the harvest in the fields around Hope Church, really aren't relevant any more. Twenty-five Presbyterian farmers, or a handful of monks for that matter, don't have much to say to the world.

And yet I wonder. I wonder if a church like Hope doesn't teach the world in the way a monastery does, not by loudly voicing its views but by existing quietly in its own place. I wonder if what Columba Stewart, a contemporary Benedictine, has said about such earthy metaphors, that "the significance of field, vineyard and garden metaphors in biblical and post-biblical texts . . . lies beyond their relevance to the agricultural economy of ancient peoples," really means that our urban civilization surpasses such metaphors at its peril. As Stewart says, "these images describe the process of human cultivation," and as such they may be an essential part of being human, and of being religious in a human way.

Does the city, any city, need Hope Church? Does America need people on the land? In the last volume of Ole Rolvaag's *Giants in the Earth* trilogy a country pastor, addressing Norwegian farmers in Dakota who are losing their "old country" ways, and in fact are eager to lose them in order to become good Americans, declares that "a people that has lost its traditions is doomed." He adds:

> If this process of leveling down, of making everybody alike . . . is allowed to continue, America is doomed to become the most impoverished land spiritually on the face of the earth; out of our highly praised melting pot will come a dull . . . smug complacency, barren of all creative thought . . . Soon we will have reached the perfect democracy of barrenness . . . Dead will be the hidden life of the heart which is nourished by tradition, the idioms of language, and our attitude to life. It is out of these elements that character grows.

The process of acculturation to American life has traditionally been accelerated in cities; it takes more time for rural people to change. But Rolvaag's pastor is as relevant as the contemporary debate about multiculturalism. "If we're to accomplish anything worthwhile," he says, "we must do it as Norwegians. Otherwise we may meet the same fate as corn in too strong a sun."

I wonder if roles are now reversed, and America's urban majority, native born or not, might be seen as immigrants to a world of asphalt and cement, and what they need more than anything is access to the old ways of being. Access to the spirits of land and of place. The image of a democracy of barrenness rings true when one turns on the television and finds bland programs designed for the widest possible audience, or when one drives a busy freeway or walks through an airport parking garage, places that are no place, where you can't tell by looking if you are in Tulsa or Tacoma, Minneapolis or Memphis.

The sense of place is unavoidable in western Dakota, and maybe that's our gift to the world. Maybe that's why most Americans choose to ignore us. Upward mobility is a virtue in this society; and if we must keep moving on, leaving any place that doesn't pay off, it's better to pretend that place doesn't matter. But Hope Church, south of Keldron, is a real place, a holy place; you know that when you first see it, one small building in a vast land. You know it when you walk in the door. It can't be moved from where it is on the prairie. Physically, yes, but that's beside the point.

Hope's people are traditional people, country people, and they know that the spirits of a place cannot be transported or replaced. They're second-, third-, and fourth-generation Americans who have lived on the land for many years, apart from the mainstream of American culture, which has become more urban with every passing year. Hope's people have become one with their place: this is not romanticism, but truth. You can hear it in the way people speak, referring to their land in the first person: "I'm so dry I'm starting to blow," or "I'm so wet now I'll be a month to seeding."

A pastor who was raised on a farm in Kansas said he thought what made Hope special was that the members were "all, or nearly all, totally dependent on the land." He didn't seem to mind that church attendance got sparse at haying time and at calving, which is a round-the-clock operation for most ranch families; every three hours or so someone must check the pregnant heifers. The fact that this often coincides with brutal spring blizzards doesn't help; newborns can freeze to death in a matter of minutes.

"I spent some time on trail rides with Hope's ranchers," the pastor said, "and also helped at lambing. But they were a bigger help to me than I was to them. To touch the earth, the real earth, once again, restored my soul."

I once heard Martin Broken Leg, a Rosebud Sioux who is an Episcopal priest, address an audience of Lutheran pastors on the subject of bridging the Native American/white culture gap. "Ghosts don't exist in some cultures," he said, adding dismissively, "They think time exists." There was nervous laughter; we knew he had us. Time is real to us in America, time is money. Ghosts are nothing, and place is nothing. But Hope Church claims by its very existence that place is important, that place has meaning in and of itself. You're still in America in the monastery, and in Hope Church — these absurd and holy places — you're still in the modern world. But these places demand that you give up any notion of dominance or control. In these places you wait, and the places mold you.

Hope is small, dying, and beautifully alive. It's tribal in a way, as most of its members are related. But it does not suffer from tribalism, the deadening and often deadly insularity that can cause groups of people to fear or despise anyone who is not like them. I find in Hope many of the graces of a monastery, with stability of place and a surprisingly wide generosity in its hospitality.

It was hospitality that allowed the people at Hope to welcome me as a lay pastor. It was absurd for me to be giving sermons to them, the only person in the room who hadn't been to church in the past twenty years. I had little experience of the Bible apart from childhood memories; no training in either Scripture studies or homiletics. What could I possibly say to these people about scriptures they had been absorbing all their lives?

I did what I could, and my long apprenticeship as a poet served me well. I didn't preach much, in the traditional sense of the word; instead I stayed close to those texts, talking about the stories I found there and how I thought they might resonate with our own stories. And I got some thoughtful and encouraging response. I followed the lectionary for discipline, but got a laugh one Sunday when I mentioned that I'd chosen to ignore the advice I'd found in a guide for pastors, that one shouldn't try to connect the Old Testament, Gospel, and Epistle texts but concentrate instead on one brief passage. I said that telling a poet not to look for connections is like telling a farmer not to look at the rain gauge after a storm.

Preaching sermons was a new and unnerving experience for me, and having the people at Hope to work with was my salvation. They made it easier for me to do in those sermons what I saw I had to do, that is, disclose myself in ways different from those I was used to, hiding behind the comfortable mask of fiction. The "I" in a poem is never me — how could it be? But the "I" in my sermons came closer to home, and that was risky. "That's why we appreciated you," one Hope member told me.

I got to try out my sermons first at Hope, as the Sunday morning service there is at 9:00 A.M. and the one in town is at 11:00 A.M. More than once I finished at Hope by asking, "Can I get away with saying this in town?" Once a woman replied,

"That depends on how much faith you have," which was a good answer, as the Gospel text that day was the story of Jesus hollering at his disciples in the middle of a storm, "Why are you so afraid?" The church in town had been through a stormy period a few years back, and my sermon was an attempt to help put those bad times to rest. I knew that if I had misjudged, I would only stir things up again.

I began to find that Hope Church opened doors for me the way that Benedictine monasteries had, and it offered similar surprises. Every time I read the Scriptures aloud in the Sunday service at Hope I became aware of sparks in those texts that I had missed in preparing my sermon, and that was a wonderful experience for a poet to have, as it said much about the power of words to continually astonish and invigorate us, and even to surpass human understanding.

Monks, with their conscious attempt to do the little things peaceably and well — daily things like liturgy or chores, or preparing and serving meals — have a lot in common with the farmers and ranchers of Hope. Both have a down-to-earth realism on the subject of death. Benedict, in a section of his *Rule* entitled "Tools for Good Works," asks monks to "Day by day remind yourself that you are going to die," and I would suggest that this is not necessarily a morbid pursuit. Benedict is correct in terming the awareness of death a tool. It can be humbling, when we find ourselves at odds with another person, to remember that both of us will die one day, presumably not at one another's hands. If, as Dr. Johnson said, "the prospect of being hanged in the morning wonderfully concentrates the mind," recalling our mortality can be a healthy realism in an age when we spend so much time, energy, and money denying death.

But maybe denying death is something people need to do.

One might even look at a medieval cathedral as an expression of that need. Those buildings, however, were also made for celebrating life with music and art, with the play of light and shadow on stone and colored glass. They are beautiful in ways that modern exercise machines and lifestyles leading to that tofu-in-the-sky are not.

Tofu is still a novelty at Hope; people there obtain their protein from animals they raise on land that is suitable for nothing else. I learned at Hope Church just how profoundly the activities of farming and ranching, working the land and working closely with animals, affect the way people approach matters of life and death. Preaching in both a town and a country church, I found that the hard texts of Advent — texts about waiting, about judgment and last things — were accepted in the country while in town there was already pressure to start celebrating Christmas.

When the great wheel of the lectionary came round to the text in Isaiah that begins, "Comfort ye, comfort ye my people," and reminds us that "all flesh is grass," I preached a sermon at Hope that attempted to address the meaning of Advent in terms of the tangle of pain and joy we feel in preparing for birth and death. The town church had opted for no sermon that day. Instead, we sang Christmas carols and listened to sentimental poems from *Ideals* magazine. That text from Isaiah was read aloud during the service, but its meaning was clouded by cheer. We were busy comforting ourselves and had no wish to be reminded of our mortality.

The difference between the two churches on that Sunday confirmed what I had begun to suspect: the people of Hope Church were less afraid than the people in town to look into the heart of their pain, a pain they share with many monasteries, which also have a diminishing and aging population. When these people ask, "Who will replace us?" the answer is, "who knows, maybe no one," and it's not easy to live with that truth. The temptation is to deny it or to look for scapegoats. The challenge is to go on living graciously and thankfully, cultivating love. Not sentimental love but true charity, which, as Flannery O'Connor said, "is hard and endures."

The people of Hope live far apart from each other on the land: paradoxically, I suspect this is one reason they seem better at creating community than people in town, better at being together while leaving each other alone, as I once heard the monastic ideal defined. How are we to get along with our neighbor in hard times and good? How can we make relationships that last? Those who live in small rural communities, who come to know their neighbors all too well over the years, know the truth of the words of a sixth-century monk, Dorotheus of Gaza: "The root of all disturbance, if one will go to its source, is that no one will blame himself." When I read those words in a sermon at Hope Church, one old farmer forgot himself; he nodded and said aloud, "That's right." He was assenting to a hard truth, one confirmed by a lifetime of experience.

"All flesh is grass" is a hard truth, too, and it has real meaning for people who grow grass, cut it, bale it, and go out every day in winter to feed it to cows. They watch that grass turning into flesh, knowing that they in turn will eat it as beef. They can't pretend not to know that their flesh, too, is grass. And they know that grass dies, not just in the winter, but in summer's dry heat. "All flesh is grass, and its beauty is as the flower of the field." That image comes alive in the West River of Dakota, and also an image from Psalm 90 that speaks of "grass that springs up in the morning" and "by evening withers and fades."

It's hard for me to imagine Hope Church dying, almost impossible to picture it abandoned or falling into ruins, as human constructions inevitably do. Absurdly, I think of its death the way I think of our sun dying. Eventually, long after anyone is around to see it, the sun will grow redder and perhaps more beautiful before it finally burns out. The Grand River will have turned to ice by then, and Black Horse Butte may be stripped of its skin of grass and soil.

It's absurd, too, that I find a Benedictine monastery and a tiny Presbyterian church in the middle of nowhere to be so absolutely and perfectly complementary. I am not showing due respect to religion as I was taught it: as a matter of the fine points of who's in, who's out, who's what as defined by dogmatic and denominational distinctions. But then, I don't have to. This is the Wild West. Out at Hope, in the summer, bellowing cows at a nearby watering tank sometimes join in the call to worship; one year baby rattlesnakes showed up for Vacation Bible School.

One former minister at Hope who had come from the urban East told me that her strongest memory of Hope Church was of an evening service in July. Standing in the pulpit she could see down the length of the church and out the open door to a large round hay bale catching the last rays of sunlight. "It was dark on one side and pure gold on the other," she said, "and I thought, that's a measure of the wealth here, that will help make things come out right this year."

She also told me that she couldn't imagine what was happening at the first funeral service she conducted for a member of

Hope Church when, as people gathered for the graveside service, the men, some kneeling, began studying the open grave. It was early November, and someone explained that they were checking the frost and moisture levels in the ground. They were farmers and ranchers worried about a drought. They were mourners giving a good friend back to the earth. They were people of earth, looking for a sign of hope.

IN THE OPEN

> There was a [hermit] who was grazing with the antelopes
> and who prayed to God, saying, "Lord, teach me some-
> thing more." And a voice came to him, saying, "Go into
> this [monastery] and do whatever they command you."
> He went there and remained in the [monastery],
> but did not know the work of the brothers. The young
> monks began to teach him the work of the brothers and
> would say to him, "Do this, you idiot," and "Do that,
> you old fool." And suffering he prayed to God, saying,
> "Lord I do not know the work of men, send me back to
> the antelopes." And having been freed by God, he went
> back into the country to graze with the antelopes.
> — *The World of the Desert Fathers*

THERE ARE AN ESTIMATED 5,000 antelope in Perkins County,
South Dakota, and about 3,900 people. Antelope are like grace
notes on the land: small and quick and bold. When threatened
they take the high ground. They confounded Meriwether
Lewis when he and William Clark first encountered them near
the White River in September of 1804:

> We found the Antelope extremely shye and watchfull . . . I
> got within about 200 paces of them when they smelt me and
> fled; I gained the top of the eminence on which they stood,
> as soon as possible from whence I had an extensive view of
> the country the antilopes which had disappeared in a steep
> reveene now appeared at a distance of about three miles on

the side of a ridge — so soon had these antelopes gained the distance I doubted at ferst that they were the same I had just surprised, but my doubts soon vanished when I beheld the rapidity of their flight . . . it appeared reather the rappid flight of birds.

Seeing antelope bound across a field quickens my heart; I long to go with them. It's like the feeling I used to have when I was a kid playing outdoors, that I never wanted to go in, that I could stay outside and somehow become part of that world; grass, wind and trees, day and night itself.

I get that feeling now when I'm in the open, walking in the country around my prairie town. The land, the 360 degrees of unobstructed horizon, invites you to keep on walking. The light is continually changing: shadows of cloud move fast on the land, coloring it slate blue. A sudden break in the cloud cover turns a butte chalk white; a cloudburst in the distance unleashes sheets of rain, and you study it carefully for the telltale white sheen that means hail. A person could stand and watch this changing land and sky forever.

Even on very cold days (and my gauge for that is an informal one: if my eyebrows start to ache, it's below zero), coming back into a house feels all wrong. It is hard to turn back to the human world of ceiling and walls and forced air heating.

I know the shock of hitting paved road after riding grass-track roads and walking in the country all day. The rhythm of the tires on the two-lane blacktop says to me: *civilization, town, other people,* and I don't want that. As when I was a child, I want to remain in the open, becoming something other than human under the sky.

Maybe it's our sky that makes us crazy. We can see the

weather coming, and we like it that way. Being truly of the Plains, however, means something more. It's the old North Dakota farmer asked by a sociologist why he hasn't planted trees around his farmhouse. No shelterbelt, not even a shade tree with a swing for his children. "Don't like trees," he said, "they hem you in."

BLESSING

MONASTERIES ARE MADE FOR WALKING, and I think this accounts for much of the peace people find in them. Here, in winter, when ice and the north wind make walking outside difficult, the long corridors and tunnels connecting the monastery, church, dining room, and library provide ample opportunity for walking, for meditating, for listening to the body's rhythms.

One night in spring, vespers ended with the whole community walking solemnly, to the slow pace of a litany, through the church and out the front door to the garden. The gardeners led us, carrying a processional cross, incense, and a few seedlings to be blessed. The cantors and the abbot brought up the rear.

We called on the angels, and Saint Isidore, patron of farmers. The long skirts of the monks' habits kept time: "From all evil, deliver us O Lord; from drought and pestilence, deliver us O Lord." When we got to the garden we made a circle and the abbot led us in prayers, sprinkling holy water on the plants, on the well-weeded soil, and on us. In the wind the monks' scapulars made a sound like the wings of the nighthawks wheeling above.

This ritual is one of the most ancient known to humankind. In some parts of Europe an icon of the Black Madonna, her skin as dark as the ploughed soil, is still carried around the fields before planting. No matter what one believes in, there is something wonderful about blessing things. If they hold to tradition, this community will perform this ceremony in reverse in early autumn, carrying the garden's first fruits to the church to be blessed, and proceeding on to the kitchen, blessing it, the utensils, and the cooks for good measure.

The ceremony put us in a good mood. We stood in small groups, visiting. With the blue light of dusk came the smell of rain. A few drops; not enough to make much difference, but something. Bats began shooting from the pottery building to the monastery proper and the novice, a shy and bearish young man, picked a sprig of lilac to take to his room. He lumbered off with it, holding it close to his chest, the purple made more vivid by the severe black of his habit. "Take more," an old monk called to him. "Take more."

Weather Report: September 3

◆

I am too late for dawn light, *morgenrud;* the eastern sky is the color of burnished gold. Today I am a judge of gardens. I pass by the haunted backyards of Gertrude's sweet, crooked smile and Esther's lopsided, arthritic walk. Their gardens are gone now, replaced by lawns and wooden decks, their fruit trees buried under the foundations of ranch houses built on the western edge of town.

Turning back east, I pass the rural Lutheran parsonage. He has too much shade; the corn won't amount to much. But a squash is ablaze with blossom — maybe he'll get something there. I recall a saying of the desert monks: "If a man settles in a certain place and does not bring forth the fruit of that place, the place itself casts him out."

MY MONASTICISM

I WAS RECENTLY AFFORDED the unusual privilege of joining a Benedictine community in North Dakota for its annual retreat. The community is a large one, over one hundred women, many of whom work outside the convent. They are nurses, social workers, chaplains, professors. Like many modern Benedictines, they try to strike a balance between the active and contemplative life, and once a year they make a retreat that returns them to the stillness at the heart of monasticism. One sister described it as drawing water from an inexhaustible well.

The retreat schedule was simple and livable, reflecting a moderation that is typically Benedictine. Morning prayer at 7:00, followed by breakfast; a conference or talk by the retreat director from 9:00 to 9:30; Eucharist at 11:00, followed by lunch; mid-day prayer at 1:00; coffee (optional) at 2:00; from 3:00 to 3:30 a second conference; vespers at 5:00 followed by dinner. Free time allowed for walks, reading, private prayer, naps, and assigned work, such as setting tables.

The most wonderful thing about all this is that it was conducted without any chit-chat. I am a frequent guest at several monasteries on the Great Plains that follow silence at certain hours, but I had never before immersed myself in the kind of silence that sinks into your bones. I felt as if I were breathing deeply for the first time in years.

To live communally in silence is to admit a new power into your life. In a sense, you are merely giving silence its due. But this silence is not passive, and soon you realize that it has the power to change you. I've gained a new respect for my more contemplative friends, Cistercians and Trappists; to live this kind of silence, day in, day out, must be an act of bravery.

During the retreat even meals were held in silence, with the ancient monastic practice of table reading. As we ate, a sister read to us from an excellent essay on ecology. Meals in common were holy to Saint Benedict, and Benedictine life aims for continuity between church and dining hall, a continuity that silence tends to amplify. As we scraped and stacked our dishes I noted that, as is usual with monastic people, very little food was wasted. You take what you need and eat what you take. The article reminded us that we all have a long way to go, but we could see that there was a connection between what we had been praying in church and practicing at our meal.

The meal also reflected the profound humility before nature evident in the earliest Christian monastics that has endured in religious life for over 1,500 years. Like mystics, monastic people have often been a counterweight in a religion that has often denigrated nature. Modern monastics are more fully grounded in the natural world than many who live in the rat-race, measuring time in sound bites or thirty-second commercials. Even urban monasteries run on a rural rhythm, taking notice of sunrise and sunset with morning prayer and evensong.

As a writer I was intrigued by the conferences presented during the retreat, pithy talks on the life and ministry of Jesus given by a monk who teaches in a Benedictine seminary. I once heard him address a general audience on monastic history. But his retreat talks were not lectures; instead they were true to what Benedicta Ward has termed the essence of the ancient desert monks' spirituality, that which "was not taught but caught; it was a whole way of life." The retreat conferences were soundings that could only have come from someone who has lived as a monk for many years, practicing *lectio divina,* the Benedictine term for meditative reading. Coming out of the depths of silence, these talks elicited a response that could only lead back to silence.

I've done many poetry readings in my life, and have attended countless more. I've also sat through sermons. Never had I experienced anything like this. The talks, preceded by ten or fifteen minutes of recollection, in which presenter and audience sat together in silence, were held in the church where we had Mass and common prayer. The space provided continuity and deepened our listening. Paying attention became a serious matter. "Listen" is the first word of Benedict's *Rule* and of course it is silence that makes listening possible.

Ora et labora, pray and work, is a Benedictine motto, and the monastic life aims to join the two. This perspective liberates prayer from God-talk; a well-tended garden, a well-made cabinet, a well-swept floor, can be a prayer. Benedict defined the liturgy of the hours as a monastery's most important work: it is, as the prioress explained it, "a sanctification of each day by common prayer at established times." Many people think it's foolish to spend so much time this way, but the experience of Benedictines over 1,500 years has taught them that doing anything else is unthinkable. It may be fashionable to assert that all is holy, but not many are willing to haul ass to church four or five times a day to sing about it. It's not for the faint of heart.

My monasticism is an odd one. It's not play-acting, though

I've wondered about that at times. It isn't even a case of what monks call "Benedictine-wanna-be." No matter how much liturgy I attend with my monastic friends, I am not vowed to their communities, and that's what counts. But through the grace of Benedictine hospitality I have felt welcomed to church for the first time since I was a child. Theirs is in fact a childlike church, though it's anything but childish. Monks sing a good deal, they listen to stories without much interpretation, and despite (or perhaps because of) their disciplined lives, they seem more at ease with their faith than most other Christians I've met, tending to live it quietly rather than proselytize. What began as a strong attraction — the first time I visited a monastery, I dreamed about it every night for a week — has slowly developed into something deeper.

I come and go from the monastery, of course, and when I leave I try to carry with me some of its peace. As I often depart by Greyhound Bus, I face an immediate challenge. One day in spring I left the monastery reluctantly. The winter had been hellish and I was exhausted. The last thing I wanted was a long bus ride to a conference where I'd have to be sociable. I hugged my monk friends goodbye, boarded the bus and collapsed into a seat. Glancing across the aisle, I was greeted by an incarnation of Psalm 131, which we'd read aloud at vespers the night before: "like a weaned child on its mother's breast, even so is my soul." A young woman, a poor young woman, to judge by her shabby clothes and traveling case, had dozed off with a small child asleep on her breast. Mother and child presented a perfect picture of peace.

Welcome to the world, I told myself; I hope I know a blessing when I see one. Later, when a young couple nearby began necking as I came across a passage from *The Song of Songs* in my breviary, I thought: how perfectly blessed we are. The bus sped on along the interstate, and I began to miss my husband, and as the couple's kisses gave way to a sleepy cuddling, the monk within me sang the praises of all the simple pleasures.

God Is in the Details: Winter Wheat

———◆———

She said, "Well, you seed it in September. And it comes up
right away. Then it dies back down and you hope for a good
snow cover. If there's been enough moisture it comes back up
in April, around Easter."

Weather Report: October 2

◆

"When my third snail died," the little girl writes, sitting half-way in, halfway out of her desk, one leg swinging in air, "I said, 'I'm through with snails.' " She sits up to let me pass down the aisle, the visiting poet working with the third grade: in this dying school, this dying town, we are writing about our lives. I'm hungry, looking forward to the lefse I bought for lunch at the Norwegian Food Festival sponsored by the Senior Citizen Center, one of the few busy places on Main Street. That and the post office, the café, the grocery. The other buildings are empty.

The teacher's writing too. Yesterday she told me that when I asked the kids to make silence and the room was suddenly quiet, she thought of her mother. "She's been dead for years," she said, adding almost apologetically, "I don't know why I thought of her. But then I just had to write." She told me about the smells, how this time of year the lingering scent of pickling spices in the house would gradually give way to cinnamon, peppermint, cloves, the smells of Christmas baking. "It was the candy I loved most," she wrote, "nut fudge, caramels, divinity."

The sunsets here have been extraordinary, blazing up like distant fire in the window of the old boarding house where the school has put me. Last night I was reading when the light changed: I looked up and gasped at the intensity of color, a slash of gold and scarlet on the long scribble of horizon.

I was reading one of the old ones who said, "One who keeps death before his eyes conquers despair." The little girl calls me, holding up her paper for me to read:

> When my third snail died, I said,
> 'I'm through with snails.'
> But I didn't mean it.

IS IT YOU, AGAIN?

V ISITS TO MONASTERIES ARE as old as monasteries themselves. We think of monks as being remote from the world, but
Saint Benedict, writing in the sixth century, notes that a monastery is never without guests, and admonishes monks to "receive all guests as Christ." Monks have been quick to recognize
that such hospitality, while undoubtedly a blessing, can also
create burdens for them. A story said to originate in a Russian
Orthodox monastery has an older monk telling a younger one:
"I have finally learned to accept people as they are. Whatever
they are in the world, a prostitute, a prime minister, it is all the
same to me. But sometimes I see a stranger coming up the road
and I say, 'Oh, Jesus Christ, is it you again?' "

From the beginnings of Christian monasticism, hospitality
has been seen not only as an important part of a monk's spiritual discipline, but as a way in which the monk lives out the
Gospels, incarnating the openness Jesus shows to all people,
even the cast-offs of society. But tension is built into the relationship between host and guest, and the desire to protect the
peace and solitude of their life has often made monks look at
guests with a wary eye. As early as the fourth century, visitors
to desert monks in Egypt reported that they distinguished
between "guests from Jerusalem and guests from Egypt." They
offered hospitality — food and a place to rest — to both, but

only the former were invited to stay and share in the life. The tourists were blessed and sent on their way.

The monk mystique has kept visitors coming over the centuries, and they often return with glimpses of the life that contradict the popular image of the monk, but don't make him any less mysterious. An eighteenth-century visitor to an Egyptian monastery recorded this chaotic worship service: "Frequently, they do not know what they ought to sing; one would have this anthem or psalm, another would have that, on which a dispute arises which comes to blows, while a third chants a prayer."

The stories outsiders bring back are often very moving. Robert, Lord Curzon, visiting Mount Athos in the 1830s, stayed overnight in a shepherd's hut, and heard the monk's story. Orphaned in a Romanian uprising, the monk was brought to the monastery as a young boy. "He did not remember his mother," Curzon writes, "and did not seem quite sure that he had ever seen a woman. He asked me whether they resembled the pictures of the Panagia, the Holy Virgin, which hang in every church."

Sacheverell Sitwell, visiting European monasteries in the 1920s to study their architecture, takes the modern sophisticate's view of monks as anachronisms, medieval relics rattling around in the twentieth century, yet he notes: "There is sympathy for their lives of religious conviction and tranquillity, and a curiosity that could become a longing for what is perhaps only latent in us and not lost." This longing, I believe, is a key to the attraction monks and monasteries hold for us.

The attraction is real. For all our secular preoccupations, our fascination with lifestyles of the rich and famous, twentieth-century Americans are flocking to monasteries for retreats in record numbers. The poor and humble are so popular, in fact, that when I tried a few years ago to arrange on short notice a retreat at a monastery in New England, I was told by an apologetic monk that the guest facilities were booked solid for the next six months.

In recent years both *Harper's Bazaar* and *Forbes* have published articles suggesting that their readers take to monasteries for rest and relaxation. Monastic retreat centers are sometimes featured in the travel sections of Sunday papers. Monks don't necessarily mind this, as some of these guests from Egypt will turn out to be guests from Jerusalem in disguise. But often it's hard for monks to understand that people coming in from the noise of the world are so impressed by the relative quiet of the monastery that they see a paradise where there is none, and imagine monks to be more angelic than not. Monks are symbols of such a deep human longing that, paradoxically, others often have trouble seeing them as human beings. This is a complaint monks will make to anyone who will listen. "If another person says, 'It's so peaceful here,' I'll scream," one monk said to me.

I suspect that monastic life is like marriage in that only those on the inside really know what's going on. But outsiders keep trying to make sense of monasteries, with varying degrees of success. A *Newsweek* reporter captured the essence of the communities I've encountered, saying that "Despite their doubts and foibles, these . . . are special people. Some are sophisticated and scholarly, others are earthy and well-balanced, a few are simply God's fools." In summary he said, "I sensed much happiness behind these walls."

Sometimes monks themselves can be prevailed upon to give a good assessment of the life. In a revealing quote in *U.S. News & World Report* a Trappist says,

> there is no way you could give a rational explanation of this way of life . . . The reasons you stay are not the reasons you enter. It is easy to get caught up in the externals like the vegetarian diet and getting up at 3 A.M. — as if we were "a few good men" like the Marines. But gradually you find that the important thing is the development of inner peace and growth that comes with experiencing God.

Monks know, as one Benedictine recently put it, without complaint, that "people want to see Christ in us." They are aware, however, that this very expectation makes them vulnerable to the outsider's perception of them as holy men. Because they represent an archetype of holy simplicity, others may use them as ciphers on which to project their hopes and fears. A particularly revealing article in this regard appeared several years ago in *The Christian Century,* entitled "My Close Encounters with Monasticism."

Admitting to a "flagrantly romantic ideal," the author speaks of poring over photographs of medieval monasteries as evidence of "an insatiable longing for the contemplative life." He's a modern, middle-class American, though, and wants a quick fix. Attending a liturgy at the ecumenical community of Taizé, in France, he records his high hopes: "I watched, wondering if this was to be the will of God for me." He wants fireworks and when he feels "nothing — no sign; no vision; no still, small voice calling me forth," he is perplexed. Petulantly, he writes: "I left . . . and journeyed Europe without visiting another monastery."

A few years later, at the gates of a monastery in Colorado,

where he insists that a "real and potent" attraction to the contemplative life has led him, he reports that fear kept him from entering the grounds. This could be a promising sign, but the promise is shattered in the unintentionally hilarious passage that follows. Parking by the monastery entrance, and casually referring to a monk he sees in the distance as "my alter ego," he

> [waits] for something to happen . . . I wanted to call — to hear a monk's voice; to request a retreat; to become a postulant; to find the answers to all the questions I had in my life and soul. I wanted to call for help, to say that I was ready to offer my life unconditionally to God. But I stopped there, stoically waiting and resting against the fender of my Porsche.

When two men, presumably monks, come down the drive in a pickup truck, he gets in his car and leaves. He writes, "I did not want to explain myself, to bare my soul, to cry out for mercy. I did not want to reveal my true self." Monks are used to dealing with all sorts of characters who appear at their doorsteps, but it seems to me that the deceptively simple command of Benedictine hospitality to receive all guests as Christ demands something of the guest as well. Reticence, perhaps, holding back from baring your soul at every opportunity. Monastic hospitality is essentially playful, and if one is not willing to play along, to enter the great "as if" of the divine comedy, then monks are indeed aliens with whom one can have only strange encounters. Monks are so willing to welcome strangers and give them the benefit of the doubt, it seems a shame not to respond in kind.

One contemporary visitor to monasteries who seems to have understood what Trappist Matthew Kelty has described as "the play that is at the heart of the liturgy and the contemplative life" is Alec Guinness. Monks figure prominently in his engaging autobiography, *Blessings in Disguise,* a book I heard read aloud in a monastic refectory where talk was forbidden, but laughter, thank God, was not. Guinness is respectful of the monastic liturgy as "prayer without frills" and senses that in the monastery he is "at the centre of some spiritual power-house . . . the work of a great turbine." But he is not distracted by his own angst, or by a romantic ideal of the monk.

Guinness is astonished to find on his first visit to a Trappist abbey near Leicester that the monk assigned to show him hospitality has an "almost garrulous" nature. "He asked me what I thought the most difficult part of being a monk might be. 'Other monks,' I replied promptly. He gave me a long, quizzical look of the kind Edith Sitwell was so expert at giving, and said, with some solemnity, 'Yes!' I felt I had gone to the top of the class." Perhaps Guinness's actor's instinct helped him to perceive the ordinary human being underneath the severe makeup of the monastic role.

On a retreat at Subiaco, where Benedict established a hermitage after fleeing the chaos of sixth-century Rome, Guinness finds the abbot to be "a cultured, urbane man, amused by life and tolerant of his guests." The abbot is exasperated, however, by the swarm of reporters waiting outside the abbey gates on the day of the actor's departure. He and Guinness are brought back abruptly into the world by the first question that floats above the crowd: "Do you know Gina Lollabrigida?" — after Saint Benedict, Subiaco's most famous export.

Monks have long told such humbling and playful stories about themselves and the world. One of my favorites is an ancient story of a gathering of bishops in Antioch, one of whom is the monk Nonnus. He scandalizes the other men by daring to thank God for the beauty of a notorious courtesan who has ridden naked through the city. The others look away as she passes by wearing nothing but jewelry but he asks, "Did not her great beauty delight you? Truly, it delighted me." Then he chastises his fellow bishops, commenting that he only wishes he had the desire to please God that she has to please men.

To one contemporary monk, this story is at the heart of monastic contemplation, in that it calls a monk not to refuse to look at the world but to discover God at work in it. The story is also a subtle evocation of monastic hospitality as an invitation to new self-awareness. As the story goes, the courtesan heard of the monk's remark and came to him in disguise, seeking to change her life. She became a nun, and the church acquired a new saint, Pelagia the Harlot.

True hospitality is marked by an open response to the dignity of each and every person. Henri Nouwen has described it as receiving the stranger on his terms, and asserts that it can be offered only by those who "have found the center of their lives in their own hearts." Monastic life seeks to provide the silence and stillness that leads to such awareness for the individual monk and then allows him to offer it, through hospitality, to others who seek it.

For the monk, even repentance is seen in terms of hospitality. For one modern Benedictine, repentance means "not primarily . . . a sense of regret," but "a renunciation of narrow and sectarian human views that are not large enough for God's mystery." It means recognizing that we have not always seen grace where it exists in the world, and agreeing "to turn away from a stubborn and obdurate position that cannot accept what is new and different and therefore cannot entertain God's mysterious ways." The word "entertain" is used advisedly here, as the monk goes on to speak of hospitality: "The classic sign of [our] acceptance of God's mystery is welcoming and making room" for the stranger, the other, the surprising, the unlooked-for and unwanted. It means learning to read the world better, that we may better know our place in it.

I discovered monasteries after moving to the Great Plains, and the most surprising thing to me about the hospitality I found is that it is powerful without being seductive; it does not lead aside or astray, but home. It won't necessarily make you a follower or even a fan of monks; instead, it will encourage you to examine and define your own deepest commitments.

It is in this sense that monastic hospitality has made me feel part of a vast giveaway, to use a Native American term. A Lakota friend who is a Roman Catholic tells me that for her both the pipe ceremony and the Eucharist demonstrate that the gift is always moving, always being given and received. I learned that this receiving and giving of gifts moved freely across ecumenical boundaries when I found that *lectio*, a monastic practice which means, among other things, immersion in the contemplation of scripture, made it possible for me to write the sermons that several Presbyterian churches had asked of me. And in turn, writing the sermons deepened my experience of *lectio*.

But this flow of gifts was open to me only as I became open to it, through a period of doubt and testing when I wondered why I had wandered so far afield of my Protestant upbringing, why I was drawn to a community of celibate Roman Catholic men. But the gifts kept coming, despite my doubts, and gradually I realized that their hospitality was functioning as true hospitality should, helping me to become who I wanted to be as a writer, as a wife, even as a Presbyterian, and that this was as it should be.

This process was facilitated by the fact that the monasteries I visit on the Plains are not overrun by guests. Typically enough, it was on a frontier, on the margins of society, that monastic discipline was relaxed enough so the monks could be more open to me, making it easier for me to see that they were quite ordinary people. The gifts came only after I had accepted their hospitality as it is, without any preconceptions of what monks are or should be. It's convenient to stereotype monks as either oddities or holy men, but in pigeonholing them we impede their marvelous hospitality. Doors that would open remain closed, and we cheat only ourselves.

A few years ago a journalist doing an Easter story about a monastery on the Great Plains insisted that he needed a photograph of a monk with a broom. The scholarly monk who finally agreed to pose was quickly dubbed Brother Broom by his confreres as they laughed over the article at breakfast on Easter Sunday. It didn't help that the monk was misquoted in the story so that he seemed to be taking a heretical position on the Incarnation. This ludicrous situation could have been avoided, and the reporter might even have gotten a better story, had he photographed the young monk who worked the abbey's industrial vacuum. The tapes on his Walkman were of Tibetan monks he'd recorded in India, and he found it amusing that the bass tones of the monks resonated well with the deep vibrato of the vacuum. "A perfect blend," he joked, "of prayer and work."

It's hard to say what monastic people mean to us. I suppose they're a lot like poets: nice to have around until they ask to be taken seriously. What can we learn from these ordinary people who have been called to live in an extraordinary way, "testing the heart," as a ninety-year-old nun put it to me. What do we as guests mean to them? They can't see themselves as others see them, and often don't understand the effect of their other-ness on those who encounter them. Some tell me that guests are important to them because as they struggle with the daily grind in the small world of the monastery, they can lose sight of the big picture. A guest can remind a monk that the monastic life has purpose and meaning.

Sometimes this happens in a dramatic way. A few years ago a man appeared at a small Benedictine convent on the Plains and left the sisters a nearly new Jeep, its papers all in order. It had been purchased on the East Coast, and the owner had driven more than halfway across the country before he decided, on seeing the priory sign, to give it to the nuns. He had asked only that the sisters pray for him as he walked away.

The Jeep caused a minor flare-up in the community: one younger sister wanted to keep it, knowing that it would be helpful (not to mention fun) to drive on the gravel roads they often had to use. The other sisters were bent on selling it and using the money in their mission work with Native Americans. As they argued amicably, I clutched my as-yet unread *Rule* of Saint Benedict. It was my first visit to a Benedictine house and I was very much taken with these events. I had sensed that this was a grieving community. They had recently lost sev-eral members, including younger women who had left to get married. They had sold their large convent building and were housed in a former rectory.

I was astonished when one sister turned to me and asked, "Why did he give us the Jeep? I don't understand." I said, without hesitation, "It's because you people stand for something." It was then that I realized that the Jeep was a gift in the deepest sense, ennobling both giver and recipient.

The sisters had spoken with the donor and concluded that he was sane, the gesture a necessary part of some healing process in his life. I'm sure they pray for him still. But the man's gift to the women was healing for them as well. It helped restore their sense of mission, their sense of having a viable monastic community. Even the most secular person might understand that to the sisters he was indeed the guest as Jesus Christ, again.

The truly radical nature of monastic hospitality did not become clear to me until I was far from my home in South Dakota, visiting an old friend and mentor in New York City who was dying of cancer and had just weeks to live.

She asked me about the monastery I had affiliated myself with as an oblate, and said, "I like the person you're becoming." Rousing herself to sit up straight on her sofa, even though it was painful, she said, "Those monks are good for you," adding, "Don't let them forget me."

Suddenly I saw, standing in a room thousands of miles from that abbey on the Plains, what monks are for. Their hospitality allowed us to say our goodbyes and gave my friend a chance to bless me and charge me with keeping her memory. Any notion I still had of monks as otherworldly anachronisms went out the window and was lost in the Manhattan night.

If monks are crazy to live the way they do, maybe the world needs more such craziness, what Matthew Kelty has termed "the madness of great love." My narrow world had just opened wide, and I had glimpsed such a love.

Returning to the deserts of Egypt, where Christian monasticism began over 1,700 years ago, we find Coptic monasteries still flourishing. A recent visitor, Jesuit Robert Taft, reported in the *American Benedictine Review* that he found a hospitality much like that encountered by visitors in the fourth century, who told of being greeted by "monks [pouring] out of their cells like a swarm of bees [running] to meet us with delight and alacrity." The modern monks were also extremely solicitous of their visitor. When he thanked them for their assistance at liturgy, one replied, "Your presence in our choir is a blessing on all the fathers." This, the writer says,

> is but one example of the gentle courtesy that characterizes the speech and gesture of the desert monks, a courtesy some-what quaint and stylized for one accustomed to the breezy familiarity of Americans, but nonetheless appreciated. Ask for something and the monk will bring his right hand to his breast and say, "I am your servant." Thank him for showing you around and he will say, "It was a blessing to be with you." Tell them you are a professor and you will hear, "Pro-fessors are angels who announce the Good News."

This giddy sweetness may still be found in American mon-asteries, though the language is toned down. It has deep roots in the notion of God's ever-present hospitality in both nature and other people, the idea that, properly understood, every-thing in creation invites us to share in God's love. A story that eloquently expresses this may be found in the life of Benedict himself. It is said that a priest came unexpectedly to the saint's cave, bringing food. "Let us eat," he said, "for it is Easter." Benedict replied, "I know that it is Easter, for I have been granted the blessing of seeing you."

Such hospitality can't help but change both parties, and that is part of its purpose. Our curiosity about monks that, as

Sitwell said, tends toward a longing, is centered not on the monk so much as on our own possibilities for change, on "what is perhaps only latent in us and not lost." We respect the fact that monastic people have gone through a period called "formation," in which, as one Benedictine sister told me, "disillusionment is a fairly predictable outcome. But we need to be disillusioned. We need to lose our false selves."

Ironically, it is in choosing the stability of the monastery or the Plains, places where nothing ever happens, places the world calls dull, that we discover that we can change. In choosing a bare-bones existence, we are enriched, and can redefine success as an internal process rather than an outward display of wealth and power.

Maybe it's our longing for the good in ourselves that draws us to monasteries and is realized in the reciprocal gift giving of monastic hospitality. Maybe, as disillusioned adults, we first know ourselves to be good when a monk welcomes us as we are, with joyful hospitality and desire for communion. If monastic formation encourages the monk to see "Christ in our midst as well as on our altars," as one nun put it, it also encourages the guest to recognize the holiness within, to be more hospitable to the self, saying with the monk, in weariness and wonder: "Oh, Jesus Christ, is it you, again?"

Weather Report: November 2

◆

Wind prowled the monastery grounds, giving night silence an increased air of watchfulness. Glass shook in the window frames and sleep was slow in coming.

We had prayed at vespers for the deceased members of the community, from Isidore who died in 1898 to Michael who died last year. We sang of "the narrow stream of death," as if the distance were not so far. I woke to find the ground dusted with snow, the Killdeer Mountains looming white on the horizon, a distance of forty-five miles.

All Souls', blustery and chill. I hear them before I see them, six lines scribbling across the white sky. I look up at the tiny crosses beating above me. The pain is new each year, and I'm surprised, even though I expect it: the sudden cold, the geese passing over.

DUST

Kneeling in the basement, I recall the church in Enna, Sicily, where Ceres and Proserpine reigned until a pope kicked them out in the mid-nineteenth century. This is my Hades, where I find what the house has eaten: the cut-glass powder jar with silver lid my grandmother received on graduation from Sioux City High School in 1909; five sets of my grandfather's longjohns, three wool, two cotton.

I cut off the sleeves to make covers for my rolling pin.

I find my mother's piano music; she played when she was a girl. I find a receipt for $12.50, for a funeral held in 1897: my grandfather, a boy of eleven, had kept it with fragments of fabric from his mother's dresses and strands of her hair; kept it hidden for seventy-six years.

One who has followed a combine as it harvests wheat, spitting out chaff and field dirt, knows what dust is; one who has seen real estate changing hands, as they say in Dakota, topsoil churning off land that should never have been plowed, making dust storms so dense you need your fog lights; one who has tried to live amidst the archaeological deposits of an old house.

Doing the laundry, I dig. What I do must be done over and over: like laundry, like liturgy. I want to pray to Mary Magdalene, who kept a demon for every day of the week: how practical; how womanly.

My barren black cat rubs against my legs. I think of the

barren women exhorted by the Good Book to break into song: we should sing, dear cat, for the children who will come in our old age.

She rolls in dust as I finish sweeping the cement floor. I gather up the clean clothes and a worn woolen jacket in need of mending. Then I head upstairs, singing an old hymn.

MONKS AT PLAY

It is . . . a good sort of playing which is ridiculous to men,
a very beautiful sight to the angels . . . it is a joyous game.
— BERNARD OF CLAIRVAUX on the monastic life

THAT MONKS ARE BUSY PLAYING, in all seriousness and with
a grave but not morbid intensity, is something I had begun to
figure out long before I ran across these lines by Saint Bernard.
That the small Benedictine abbeys I visit on the Great Plains are
not overrun with guests helps dispense with some of the for-
malities that mark guests' relations with monks in other parts
of the world. I eat with the monks and join them in choir. At
one abbey, when the abbot is away, the guestmaster sometimes
installs me in his seat. This may be a ploy to determine if the
novices across the way are awake. At another, when I remarked
that my stereotypes had been shattered, expecting monks
would hate women, a monk replied, "You came at the right
time. We had one like that, but he died."

One day it occurred to me that the playfulness I found in so
many of the monks was in part explained by the fact that they
are indeed playing in a serious way, dressing up in their habits
for the Divine Office, singing soft hymns of praise to wake
themselves and gentle, maternal lullabies at the end of day,
following a way of life that, ancient and honorable as it is, very
much resembles a child's way of being. When I shared this

insight with an older monk, an exceptionally wise and playful gentleman, he nodded and said, "Of course it's play. If it weren't, we wouldn't still be doing it after 1,500 years."

Peter Levi says in *The Frontiers of Paradise* that monks "become like good children playing at being good." Children, of course, love to make up rules and follow them, to continually say, "as if." Monks are behaving "as if" constancy were possible in this world, and as Levi observes, "at any visitor's first entry into a monastery, time seems to stand still." He adds that "this new time-scale . . . has nothing to do with death and eternity, but involves a tranquil, unhurried, absolutely dominating rhythm" and concludes — correctly, I believe — that this liturgical "sense of time is the greatest difference between monastic life and any other."

This is an outsider's perspective, of course. Monks tell me that this seemingly peaceful life can become hectic for them. But their ability to maintain a schedule, centered on the liturgy, does set them apart from the rest of us and, over the years, submission to liturgical time can develop a playful patience that is very much at odds with worldly values. A man who has been a monk for more than fifty years told me that when he was much younger someone told the abbot a lie about him. He knew that the abbot was operating under a misapprehension, but decided that the best course was simply to go about his business, having faith that the truth of the matter would eventually surface. He seemed amused that it had taken ten years, but shrugged and said, "What's ten years to a monk?"

I have found that monastic hospitality is also playful at heart. It can be extremely subtle as well as protean, taking forms that surprise not only the guest but the host. Serious attention to hospitality can transform shy, socially awkward young men into monks who can savor the wonders of conversation, even with people who have little in common with them. Sometimes the playfulness engendered by monastic hospitality is simply irresistible. "Would you like to see Venus?" one old monk asked me and two other women, leaning out of his homemade observatory on a bright summer morning, looking very much like the Wizard of Oz in Kansas, medicine-show wagon and all.

One memorable evening I witnessed an inspired union of playfulness and a thoughtful interpretation of Benedictine hospitality in the form of a vigorous pillow fight. I was visiting an abbey with a ten-year-old girl whose parents' divorce was becoming final in the next week. She and her mother had had a rough year, and the girl was getting her first taste of joint custody, spending the summer with her father. I met her at the bus stop that morning with a monk who carried a small bouquet; he'd picked some of the summer's last roses for the girl, because her name was Rose.

The pressures on this child were considerable; among other things, she feared the possibility of having to testify in a custody hearing. I was grateful to be able to offer her a day of play: we called on the abbot, walked the abbey grounds, pulled a few weeds in a flower bed, and attended a ceremony at which a novice received his monastic name, a solemn form of play that fascinated the girl.

One young monk, extremely introverted, befriended her at lunch and came to our room after vespers. But she had become tired and whiny, and fell on her bed with exaggerated drama, clutching a pillow. As the monk got up to leave, he carried off a move that would have done Buster Keaton proud, snatching the pillow from under her head and whacking her with it. Taken by surprise, Rose was both affronted and delighted. She grabbed another pillow, stood on the bed and hit him back, and the fight was on. It continued for nearly a half hour and was marked by brilliant tactics on both sides. When the girl grabbed the monk by his scapular, he pointed out that she had merely drawn him closer, making it easier for him to hit her. She groaned and deposited one more blow to his head. He got her in the stomach.

When the two had finally had enough (I became exhausted just watching them) the monk left and we went to bed. Rose slept soundly for fourteen hours. And that was the point: to give a frightened little girl a chance to hit — and hit hard — tiring her so she couldn't help but have a good night's sleep. All she had to do was be herself, a little girl who enjoys a pillow fight. In putting the child's needs before his own, the monk was doing battle with his natural shyness. He was also having fun. It was Benedictine hospitality at its best.

One important element of play involves mimicking, and sometimes mocking, the things that grownups or superiors do. A monk who makes vestments once showed me a scarlet cassock he'd made for an archbishop, complete with tassels on a long cord belt. He said, quietly, "I held these like a microphone when I wore this for Halloween." He had emceed the abbey's costume party, and as in true play, his act contained an underlying seriousness. Religious life, as lived experience, draws more from the well of emotions than from abstractly reasoned theologies and church structures. As one sister has pointed out, Benedictines predate the establishment of the Catholic hierarchy, and have often had a certain disdain for the princes of the church. Gently mocking them at Halloween is a playful form of an attitude that has a long history. She said, speaking of the relationship between Benedictines and the Vatican,

"We're a very decentralized order, and the popes don't like that, because when they want to tell us what to do, they can't find us."

Because they do the liturgy every day, morning, noon, and night, monastic people often develop a relaxed attitude about the holy that can alarm the more rigidly pious. On a major feast day at a Mass held jointly with a parish congregation, the monk who handed the full offering bowl to an acolyte (another monk) whispered, "Don't spend it all in one place." The game, of course, is to carry on with a straight face. Once I was enjoying the silence before vespers when a monk in the row of choir stalls behind me leaned over and whispered, "Could you keep it down?" To me, monastic choirs, for all the discipline that is in evidence, seem as open and free as country churches on the Plains. Both monks and country people take for granted that prayer works, and that it's worth doing. Why not relax and enjoy it? Why not make it beautiful?

I find the monastic sense of play pervasive even at the most unlikely times. I once spent the last week of Lent at a monastery on the Plains. Who would think to look for play at such a time and place? Yet I found it. The evening meal began with a prayer and a reading from the *Rule* of Saint Benedict, executed and received with due reverence. But the reading that followed, a witty chronicle of the monastery's early years, provided much occasion for merriment. The postulant who had fallen off the roof on his first day of work was still there, though, as the chronicle noted, he had soon been given a desk job. Other tales were of monks now deceased but still well remembered in the community. All monasteries have their characters, and in taking to heart Benedict's admonishment to "support with the greatest patience one another's weaknesses in body or behavior," monks often sense that their homes are the last refuge of the eccentric.

The meal ended with a reading from Alec Guinness's autobiography and a prayer, and shortly thereafter we filed back into church for vespers. The play in a monastery makes of life a continuous flow: church, refectory, workplace, church. Each place has its prayers and rituals, linking each activity as part of a whole. One feels part of a story that is continually unfolding, being told and retold. Even the Benedictine motto, *orare est laborare*, insisting that work *is* prayer, is to my mind an essentially playful attitude, one that may help account for the youthful countenances of so many monastics.

The Guinness autobiography provided cause for concern among several monks worried about the confrere who would next be reading from the book. A racy section was coming up and they knew he would blush and stammer. No one suggested this, but I wondered if the presence of a woman guest would make it harder for him. A small delegation looked over the text to suggest a passage he could read without difficulty, and one monk said, "it's just that he has trouble with the four-letter words, like 'penis' in that next paragraph." "Brother," another monk said solemnly, and to much effect, "penis is not a four-letter word."

Of course our laughter came, as all true humor does, from a displacement of context. A bunch of monks and a woman laughing, in the dregs of Lent, because the word penis has five letters. Is such a story an example of twentieth-century monastic decadence, or does it in fact have something to do with the observance of Lent? In some ways the monks were merely following Jesus's teaching against fasting with a gloomy face. Benedict called on monks to live a perpetual Lent, yet he made rest and reading part of their schedule, and modern monasteries usually have a daily period of communal recreation.

Here we approach the balance that is at the heart of monastic life. What do monks have to do with recreation, with fun? Benedictines regard all time as holy and seek to use it well. The point is not to avoid having fun but to keep in balance one's need for food, work, prayer, rest, and play. Moderation is essential, for, in the words of Amma Syncletica, a fourth-century desert nun, "lack of proportion always corrupts." The fact that such balance is considered ascetic says a great deal about our consumer culture. After my first stay in a monastery, where I saw Saturn and its rings through a telescope and watched monks tend their apple orchard and the garden that provides many of their winter vegetables, I happened to go directly to a shopping mall. It was easy to see which was the more unhealthy, otherworldly environment; which place was out of balance and which was, in fact, the most fun.

Still, even in the relatively liberal monasteries I visit, the perpetual Lent is much in evidence. Talk to almost any novice six months into the life. They're "bored shitless" (I'm quoting), and feel terribly constrained, confined. For good or ill, they become almost unbearably aware of the little things as they move more fully into the community, experiencing a daily familiarity with other people that is usually found only in family life. Their struggle to learn to tolerate other people's foibles often reflects what one sister termed Benedict's insight that "living in community is the only asceticism you need." This is not a shallow remark: for the Benedictine, celibacy itself is part of one's commitment to the community, eschewing love affairs that would disrupt and diminish the communal bonds a monastery seeks to maintain.

Gradually the novice discovers that a forced observation of little things can also lead to simple pleasures. A young monk once told me he'd been delighted to find that the worn black wool of the habit he'd been given was excellent for sliding down banisters. He demonstrated, and for a moment became an angel: without feet, all irrepressible joy.

It's when novices move toward survival, embracing the deprivations of monastic life as a personal, inner necessity, that they begin to feel truly free. They also begin to understand the depths of joy, and how little it has to do with what the world calls happiness. Like the farmer or rancher who willingly takes on economic hardship, remaining in Dakota out of love for the land, these monks can grow to a profound understanding of fast and feast. One makes sense only in terms of the other, and both may be seen in terms of play. Like country folk everywhere, monks develop an ability to party simply but well. "No one celebrates like we do," says Benedictine Joan Chittister in a recent commentary on the *Rule*.

I experienced the deep connection between fast and feast, gravity and play, at that abbey during Lent. Perhaps the great silence of the monastic night always seems deeper then. But as dark descended on our little ark, our feast of laughter became a remembered joy, a small bit of light and warmth that one could hope to return to. The silence of the present moment was awe-inspiring in its power, oceanic was the word that came to mind, as it carried away everything in its path. The flow of our liturgy had become one with nature's incessant movement from light to dark and back again. Such are the thoughts that comfort children, and Benedict reminds us, toward the end of the *Rule*, that we are all beginners.

It seemed appropriate that the week I spent at that abbey was the magical time in early spring when the land greens. When I arrived the grasses were thatched, bleached, beaten down; when I left, the bright green of new grass predominated. The year turned out to be a difficult one: a good friend and mentor died of cancer, my husband had a serious operation and a long, slow recovery. What little financial security we had disappeared like smoke. But it was the play as much as the piety of the monks that inspired me and helped me to survive. We had eaten together, laughed, sung psalms, inhabited silence, and played out in liturgy the entrance of Jesus into Jerusalem. All of it could be summoned up, on my darkest days, as a reminder of the rich play life could be.

Play so powerful that it can absorb adults, becoming their way of life, may have a meaning that children's play lacks. While there is an analogy between a child calling a chair a horse and a priest changing bread and wine into the body and blood of Christ, there is also a difference. In play, we create and manipulate the rules; in liturgy we act out something that has been handed down to us, and in making it our own we are also responding to the *mysterium tremendum.* Taking the playful aspects of liturgy into account, we need also to recognize the utterly serious attitudes and intentions of those involved, and the serious effect it has on them. For the monk the play of liturgy is a means of conversion, a way of life. In its deeper satisfactions it confers an abiding sense of peace.

What sets monks apart from the rest of us is not an overbearing piety but a contemplative sense of fun. They know, as Trappist monk Matthew Kelty reminds us, that "you do not have to be holy to love God. You have only to be human. Nor do you have to be holy to see God in all things. You have only to play as a child with an unselfish heart." The play of monks comes out of what I earlier termed an inner necessity; the humble acknowledgment that, for them, the liturgy must be a daily affair, a chore. They need to act it out, making the circle, singing and saying and hearing the words again and again, as a child asks to hear a beloved story many times over.

One of the first things I noticed on my longer retreats, when I was with the monks in choir four or five times a day for a week or more, was how like an exercise class the liturgy seemed. It was sometimes difficult to rise early for morning office; at other times during the day it seemed tedious to be going back to church, but knowing that the others would be there made all the difference. Once there, the benefits were tangible, and I usually wondered how I could have wished to be anywhere else. When I compared all this to an aerobics class, a monk said, "That's exactly right."

But monastic fidelity to the liturgy is the antithesis of narcissism. It is serious play indeed. It means that somewhere, as I write this, as you read it, people are singing Psalms and praying for us all. Knowing that most of us won't notice or care, they are making us a gift of their very lives. Here we approach the ultimate play in a monastery, the monk's sense that his being there at all is a sign of God's play with him. They kid about it; a monk who was raised down the street from the abbey says, "My parents brought me to be baptised and forgot to take me home," while another, who comes from New York, dreams of the aircraft carrier he served on in Vietnam. He transposes the monastic community onto the ship, putting some bad memories to rest. One monk was a farmer, another an electrical engineer. That they have each found this place, and can claim it as their own, is both miracle and joke.

Let us go now to monks at play, finishing dinner and enjoying a sunset. The World Series is over, and tonight, for the first time this week, there's no talk of baseball at table. A monk and guest are parrying with tales of Heloise and Abelard. The monk's face brightens, almost innocently, as he says, "It was the Benedictines who castrated him, you know." Another monk who has been enjoying the discussion rises and says, "I hate to leave you, but I have pots and pans tonight. Yet another sign," he says, sighing, "that the Parousia has not yet come." As he strides away, his scapular flutters behind him like a wink.

The monks will have recreation in the cloister; I'll walk the monastery grounds. Coyotes will begin calling in the coulees to the north. Soon, the monks, too, will begin to sing, the gentle lullaby of vespers and compline, at one with the rhythm of evening, the failing light and the rise of the moon. Together, monks and coyotes will sing the world to sleep.

Blue

◆

On the edge of the coulee, a grove of trees hard by the monks' cemetery, dark has already started its climb. In even the smallest indentations in the fields around me, shadows form that will eventually grasp the sky.

Dark rolls like the ocean this land once was, over stubble, grass, gravel, turning in the last light: gold, green, blue. Soon the land to the west will be a scroll, a long line writing itself against the flame of the sky, every branch in the shelterbelt of trees etched on the black scribble of horizon. Then all color will be gone.

As we head home in the car, the land rises and falls like waves. Farm lights twenty miles off bob up and down like the lights of ships, appearing and disappearing in the swells. The dark here, the dark above, have merged; frost is in the air like stars.

Weather Report: December 4
4:10 A.M.

———————◆———————

The stillness under stars. The sky recalls the painting I made of heaven when I was five; great blue-black swirls that I could never get dark enough.

I stand, as my grandmother once did, in the darkness by the house, the moon-shadow of a tree. Its feathery arms touch the shadow of the eaves. She was alone a lot in those early years: my grandfather traveling by horse-drawn sleigh or buckboard or Model T, making house calls in the country. "I was in good company," she always said, "worried I got, but never lonesome."

A jet passes over, blinking, on its way to cities in the East.

It is so cold it hurts to breathe. This is the side of the moon that no one sees.

Weather Report: December 7
3:00 A.M.

———————◆———————

Unable to sleep, I've been reading the words of a modern monk: "You have only to let the place happen to you . . . the loneliness, the silence, the poverty, the futility, indeed the silliness of your life."

A warm front is passing through. The great vault of sky is painted with high, feathery clouds; the ribs of a leviathan, or angels' wings.

I can no longer see my breath. I stand in the yard a long time, looking at the night.

One of the old ones was asked, "What is it necessary for the monk to be?" And he said, "According to me, alone with the Alone."

ACKNOWLEDGMENTS

During the writing of this book I received far more moral than financial support, and I wish to thank my husband, David, and my family. Also: Andy, David, and Elizabeth Beck, Gail and Sylvia Cross, Joan and Phil Curtis, Dorothy Dayton, James Elsing, Vern Goodin of the North Dakota Council on the Arts, G. Keith Gunderson, Mary Hanrahan of the Lemmon, South Dakota, Public Library, Claude and Ilene Hardmeyer, Marge Katus, Jane Kohn, Esther and Tom Lyman, Alice and Bill Main, Marie McLaughlin, Floyd Nilsen, Lucile Olien, Carolyn and Jerry Petik, Aldene Powers and the late John Powers, Marlin Schmidt, Carol Schnell, Dick Smith, Eileen, James, and Marguerite Sullivan, Bill and Leone Thornton, Donna and Verlyn Weishaar, Kathy Wyka and the Prairie Winds gang, especially Linda Hasselstrom, Wendy Mendoza, and Dan O'Brien, my colleagues at the Great Plains Institute of Theology, the interlibrary loan staff of the South Dakota State Library and the librarians at the College of Saint Benedict / Saint John's University. I am indebted in many ways to others whom I've neglected to mention, including some who might wish to remain anonymous.

Special thanks to Robert Lewis of *The North Dakota Quarterly*, who in 1985 published the essay that grew into this book; Deborah Clow of *Northern Lights*, for inspiring the "Weather Reports"; Elizabeth Hampsten of *Plainswoman*; and to William Stafford, for keeping me on his radar.

I also wish to thank my editor, Cindy Spiegel, and the Institute for Ecumenical and Cultural Research in Collegeville, Minnesota, where I made final revisions. My deepest gratitude to all of my Benedictine and Cistercian friends.

A few events in this book are composites of stories from several small Dakota towns. Some names have been changed to protect people's privacy.

NOTES

Portions of this book have appeared, sometimes in different versions, in the following publications:

"Dakota, or Gambling, Garbage, and the New Ghost Dance."
Beyond Borders, New Rivers Press/Turnstone Press, 1992.
"In the Open," "Seeing," "Weather Report: May 19." *The Christian Science Monitor*, December 10, 1991.
"The Jesus They Made for Us." *5 A.M.*, #4, 1990.
"Is It You, Again?" *Gettysburg Review*, Fall, 1992.
"My Monasticism." *Hungry Mind Review*, Spring, 1991.
"Monks at Play." *Massachusetts Review*, Spring, 1991.
"Gatsby on the Plains." *North Dakota Quarterly*, Autumn, 1985.
"The Beautiful Places," "Weather Report: April 14," "Weather Report: August 9," "Weather Report: September 3." *Northern Lights*, January, 1990; Spring, 1990; Fall, 1990; October, 1989.

Sources for stories of the desert monks:

Pages 17, 123, 132, 182. Thomas Merton, ed. *The Wisdom of the Desert* (New York: New Directions, 1970).
Pages 42, 98, 177, 190, 220. Columba Stewart O.S.B., ed. *The World of the Desert Fathers*. (Oxford, England: SLG Press, 1986).
Pages 6, 24, 98, 155. Benedicta Ward S.L.G., ed. *The Desert Christian* (New York: Macmillan, 1975).

Quotations from:

"Sacrifice." Katharine Ellis Barrett. *The Trenchant Wind* (Cambridge, England: Heffer & Sons, 1932).

Interview with Linda Hogan. Laura Coltelli. *Winged Words: American Indian Writers Speak* (Lincoln, Nebraska: University of Nebraska Press, 1990).

Mrs. R. Vivian Hebert
1411 Rutledge Ave
Charlottesville, VA 22903